A FAITHING OAK

A FAITHING OAK

Meditations from the Mountain

Robert A. Raines

CROSSROAD · NEW YORK

Library of Congress Cataloging in Publication Data

Raines, Robert Arnold.
A faithing oak.

1. Metiations.   I. Title.
BV4832.2.R227   1982   242   82-13076
ISBN 0-8245-0524-7

ACKNOWLEDGMENTS

Biblical quotations from THE REVISED STANDARD VERSION OF THE BIBLE, Old Testament
Section, Copyright 1952; New Testament Section, First Edition, Copyright 1946; Second Edition ©
1971 by Division of Christian Education of the National Council of the Churches of Christ in the
United States of America.

Biblical quotations from THE JERUSALEM BIBLE, Reader's Edition, Doubleday and Co., Inc.,
Garden City, New York, 1966, 1967, 1968.

"Signs" (published under the title "And This Shall Be A Sign Unto You"), "Dragons and Princesses,"
"Safety and Vulnerability," and "Yesterday's Will of God" previously appeared in *Living the Questions*, Word Inc., © 1976.

Most of the prayers included in *A Faithing Oak* previously appeared in *Soundings*, Harper & Row,
© 1970.

Contents

Prayers

To Kirkridge,
the people and the place

Introduction

Since 1974 I have been living and working on a Pennsylvania mountainside. People come to Kirkridge for a few days of refreshment, learning, encouragement. There is a strange grace by which a particular individual chooses to make the pilgrimage to a given event. Within and beyond all the conscious agendas, there is the hidden movement of the Spirit. Sometimes pilgrims in transition find transformation, wounded journeyors are healed, yearning searchers are apprehended by fresh vocation. One learns to respect the significance of place, and the promise of a piece of land. In the stories of the Bible we read that seekers often went to the mountain to hear the word of the Lord. Some still do. And for some, it becomes holy ground.

These mountainside meditations and prayers breathe the smells, tastes, colors and sounds of Kirkridge — its ambiance, eccentricities, environment. Here you will find the birds of our seasons, the work of renovating our buildings, the imperatives of our peace and justice vocation, the awe of people birthing before our eyes. It is my hope that the particularity of our time and place will not be a hindrance but rather a vehicle for you in imagining your own . . . so that these words may sink into your heart and scene. Sinking words become seedlings that take root and bear the fruits of healing, hope and courage.

Most of these reflections and prayers came out of my experience of the morning: putting on the coffee, feeding the birds, gathering Bible, lectionary and journal, and sitting down for a period of reflection. Usually I read the biblical passage of the week, then lean back to let that word descend into my heart. It may have a life of its own, or it may connect with the comment of a retreatant or leader, the turning of a season, the approach of a holy day, a pressing personal or national issue. Whatever . . . when a particular word takes root and something begins to grow in me, I write in my journal, in the hope that an in-

1

sight or intention is being borne. Often there is something to live; sometimes there is something to give.

The publication of *A Faithing Oak* coincides with the fortieth anniversary of the founding of Kirkridge. It is my hope that the meditations and prayers included here may awaken a journey in you—the kind of journey we are committed to at Kirkridge. Take a journey on which the words are your companions. Let a word or phrase sink in along the way until it pierces, wakens, intrigues, confronts you. It may leap off a page or simply loiter there. Let it take its own initiative with you . . . for awhile. Roll it around in your soul until it unfolds somewhere in your life. Feel it taking root. Notice it becoming flesh. Enter upon your own experience of the morning.

ACKNOWLEDGMENTS

I want to acknowledge my appreciation to Ruth Robinson, who coined the phrase "a faithing oak," and to Richard Payne, who encouraged the gathering of these meditations into a book. I also want to acknowledge my gratitude to the retreatants, creatures of nature, and the good earth at Kirkridge, all of which have nourished, encouraged, blessed, and comforted me.

REFLECTIONS

A Faithing Oak

Let no eunuch say, "And I, I am a dried-up tree." For Yahweh says this: I will give, in my house and within my walls . . . a name better than sons and daughters . . . an everlasting name that shall never be cut off. . . .

Isaiah 56:1–8 (RSV)

In June millions of gypsy moths infested our trees: eating the leaves, browning the ridge, defoliating the forest. The last week of June a group exploring "the pilgrimage of faith" was at the Lodge. The building was crawling with gypsy caterpillars. Some wag had put up a sign: "This building defended by attack worms." But it wasn't so funny. The lone oak tree you can see through the western celtic-crossed window was leafless, lifeless, its gray, bare branches twisted by harsh winds of many winters. The oak stood there, prematurely stripped of its sheltering leaves, bereft of its firstborn tools for livelihood, a dried-up tree.

Anyone who is childless; anyone who looks back on his most fruitful days and sorrows for ebbing energies and draining hope; anyone who fears for the nation and the world a future of calamity; anyone who is stripped by Death of a community of intimacy and nurture; anyone who feels cut off from her roots and condemned to a sterile tomorrow; all for whom the season appears barren—who feel like spiritual eunuchs, bereft of our firstborn conversion, the fires of faith grown dim and cold—may sigh, "And I, I am a dried-up tree."

One morning in that last week of June, there came a shout from a woman on the Lodge deck. She called us outside to look closely at the dried-up oak, and invited us to touch its leafless fingertips. Strange little nubbins . . . buds . . . urging forth towards a second leafing. The process of refoliation had already begun! Later in the summer we would see that oak fully leafed again. We beheld a faithing oak.

We would be faithing oaks who, having known the sacrament

5

of defeat, yet stand there withered and weathered, who con-
found the odds, turn the seasons on their heads, putting forth
seeds of hope in autumn and insisting on Easter in midwinter.
What is this outrageous grace that makes a fool of infesting
Death, and raises up a faithing oak?

In his book *Basin and Range*, John McPhee writes that at the
top of Mount Everest there are marine deposits. Who is it that
can move mountains into the sea and back again? Who is it that
can reverse the nuclear arms race before Holocaust II? Who is it
looking upon the face of a loved one dying or dead, yet can look
for joy in the morning? Who is it that will seek again and again
the restoration of a dried-up friendship? Who is it that will
reverse the values of a nation where $209,000 is spent on new
china in the White House at the very moment poor children are
asked to reduce the nutrition in their lunches (feasting in the
White House/fasting for poor children)?

We would be faithing oaks bodying forth the pained wisdom
of the survivor, staking our future on the grace of refoliation,
resurrection, restoration, rebirthing.

> O Lord, we praise You for a faithing oak in the western sky, a
> tree whose bare limbs bend and bow in suffering but are not yet
> broken. On that tree is our hope and Your promise. In nuclear
> confrontation You are showing us that the only way we can love
> our children towards a safe future is by learning to love our ene-
> mies. Hawks are wheeling high now and soaring south over the
> Lodge down the ridge. O cosmic Lover, who forgets not the lil-
> ies of the field, nor devastated oaks, nor spiritual eunuchs, re-
> member us now in the time of withering leaves, that our hope
> may endure and our faith abide. Give us grace to grieve and a
> season to mourn. Even as we bend and bow, let us not be
> ashamed, but give us the name better than sons and daughters.
> O Mother-Father God, what name could be better, how could
> we know more surely that we belong to You, and share in the in-
> heritance of Your future? Yet Your grace is beyond our under-
> standing and Your glory embraces all our woes. You in whose
> arms the sorrows of Auschwitz and Hiroshima and all our pri-
> vate agonies rest, receive us now in the moment of our dying and
> birthing. Make us a forest of faithing oaks.

Eccentric Spaces

In you, Yahweh, I take shelter;
never let me be disgraced.
In your righteousness deliver me, rescue me,
turn your ear to me, make haste!

Be a sheltering rock for me,
a walled fortress to save me!
For you are my rock, my fortress;
for the sake of your name, guide me, lead me!

Pull me out of the net they have spread for me,
for you are my refuge;
into your hands I commit my spirit,
you have redeemed me, Yahweh.

God of truth, you hate
those who serve worthless idols;
but I put my trust in Yahweh:
I will exult, and rejoice in your love!

You, who have seen my wretchedness,
and known the miseries of my soul,
have not handed me over to the enemy,
you have given my feet space and to spare.

Psalm 31:1–8 (JEB)

Recently I came by the book *Eccentric Spaces* by Robert Harbison. The subject is the human imagination and the mysterious, evocative interplay between the imagination and the spaces it has made for itself to live in: gardens, rooms, buildings, streets, museums, maps, palaces, haunted houses, hill-towns, cities, even novels, paintings and symphonies. Eccentric spaces . . . reflect with me now on some meanings.

We ride on space-ship earth with people and plankton. We occupy home-space where the anatomy of family dwelling takes shape, where parents, children, spouses — and sometimes grandparents, nieces, uncles, cousins — negotiate spaces for privacy, intimacy and community. Holy days, like Christmas, invite a family in-gathering of strength, an awkward/hopeful juxtaposition

7

of generations where it is possible, although difficult, for us to respect one another's life-space.

The word *eccentric* means odd, whimsical, off-center, irregular ... and suggests particularity, nonstandard, individuated, distinctive, unique. We might imagine the kingdom of God as eccentricity of space. A coffin is an envelope for a corpse; a house is a shell for a home; a painting is a sigh on canvas; a body is the shape of a life; a face is a faith become visible — eccentric spaces all. Perhaps eccentricity is a way of being holy. Kirkridge is the eccentricity of a singular purpose imposed on a mountainside, the contours of a vision made visible, where people may recover, uncover, or discover the eccentric spaces of their lives.

Christmas is the eccentric space of God emerging on the earth: spaces of a manger, a first century Jewish man, an empty tomb, roads to Jericho, Damascus, Emmaus and to your town and mine. The Messiah comes to give us space. If, following God, our vocation is to give one another space, how do we make those gifts? A teacher gives space to her students, a parent to his children, an architect to the dwellers in her environments, a citizen to all members of the community, a human being to all creatures and trees and stones.

How does the Messiah give us space? God is a poet. God is loving us in such a way that our prosaic lives may suffer into poetry. Poetry is the distillation of prose under gracious pressure; our lives become poetic as we undergo the interplay of the freedoms of God and ourselves. Our rebirth consists in the transformation of our space. Job *undergoes* God while his friends *discuss* God. To undergo God is to have our space transformed — not without blood, sweat and tears — into our own essential, eccentric being.

There was no space in the Inn, but Christ comes to prepare space for us, to throw open the doors and windows of many mansions, to welcome us into wide open spaces of forgiveness and freedom. Christ comes to give you this day your daily space for being and becoming in the eccentricity of the Spirit, space in which to let the Word take flesh in you to carve out your calling, and let your prosaic life become a living poem in the Lord.

Sinking Into God

> Deep is calling to deep,
> as your cataracts roar;
> all your waves, your breakers,
> have rolled over me.
>
> In the daytime may Yahweh
> Command his love to come,
> And by night may his song be on my lips,
> A prayer to the God of my life!
> *Psalm 42:7–8* (JEB)

> Nicodemus said to him, "How can a man be born when he is
> old? Can he enter a second time into his mother's womb and be
> born?" Jesus answered, "Truly, truly, I say to you, unless one is
> born of water and the Spirit, he cannot enter the kingdom of
> God."
> *John 3:4–5 (RSV)*

In a sermon entitled "Sinking Eternally Into God," Meister
Eckhart, the fourteenth-century Dominican preacher, wrote,
"We should sink eternally from something into nothing, into
this One . . . let your own 'being you' sink into and flow away into God's 'being God.'"[1] Eckhart says that the way to get to the
essence of anything is to sink into it. He invites us to sink into the
vortex or whirlpool of the Spirit which is the depth of the great
ocean of Being. Sinking into God is letting go of control, security of place or identity; letting go of all our images, definitions
and projections of God. It is the *via negativa* to the God who is
unnamed, hidden, dark, Nothing.

We're afraid of sinking. "Sink or swim" expresses our fear of
drowning, being overwhelmed by despair, circumstances, the
power of others. Sinking seems to us a way into total vulnerability, a way of losing our autonomy, a way into death. Our fear of
sinking is, most deeply, fear of the holy, being taken over by Another, fear of intimacy, of risking and possibly losing the self in
the ambiguous embrace of God. It is fear of our own rebirth.

9

The psalmist cries, "Deep is calling to deep, as your cataracts roar; all your waves, your breakers, have rolled over me." Yet the rolling waves of God bear us through the birth canal into the new life of the Spirit. Sinking into God is being born anew. How does that happen? What is it like?

Sinking into God is falling into sleep, trusting ourselves into that darkness which is like the darkness of death, entering into that dreamworld which terrifies and delights us, searching in the shadows for the Dreamer.

Sinking into God is spiraling down by meditation into our inner depths, which are the depths of the universe; descending that spiral staircase down into a place of centering, deepening silence.

Sinking into God is allowing ourselves to be washed through with music, carried by a passionate flow of sound into ecstatic wonder, or gently borne upon a peaceful river of grace.

Sinking into God is yielding to the tears that come and come and keep coming, pouring endlessly out of our own sorrow and the pain of humanity and the anguish of creation; allowing these cleansing waters to roll through us until we become clear and clean.

Sinking into God is letting ourselves be lost in the joy of a beloved place: a healing lake, a cooling forest, a quieting mountain—a place where there is nurture, care and nothing to fear.

Sinking into God is sharing the suffering of others, and witnessing against the evil of the world, where there is cruelty, death and everything to fear.

Sinking into God is entrusting ourselves passionately and openly into the depth of every thing, event, relationship, experience—in the faith that God waits there in the darkness to greet us and make all things new.

Let us pray in the words of Jacob Boehme, a seventeenth-century Christian:

> I can do nothing but sink my desire into You.
> I sink wholly and completely into Your promise.
> Let it happen with me according to Your word and will.[2]
> Amen.

The Restoration of All Things

> He has let us know the mystery of his purpose, the hidden plan he so kindly made in Christ from the beginning to act upon when the times had run their course to the end: that he would bring everything together under Christ, as head, everything in the heavens and everything on earth.
>
> *Ephesians 1:9-10* (JEB)

On the fourth Sunday of Advent, 1943, from his cell in a Nazi prison, Dietrich Bonhoeffer wrote a friend:

> ...For the past week or so these words have been constantly running through my head: "Let pass, dear brother, every pain; what lacketh you I'll bring again." What does "bring again" mean? It means that nothing is lost, everything is taken up again in Christ ... transfigured in the process, becoming transparent, clear and free from all self-seeking ... Christ brings it all again as God intended it to be ... the doctrine of the restoration of all things ... derived from Ephesians 1:10 ... is a magnificent conception and full of comfort.[1]

The restoration of all things. As we move towards the year 2000, we seek, in looking forward, a birthing of hope and, in looking backward, a healing of memories. It is a comfort that God holds our failed dreams, transient joys and damaged victories ready, waiting to restore them to their original vocation. Nothing is lost; all is subject to transformation.

We who care about the decay of cities and familiar structures may consider together the restoration of buildings. Restoration work was begun in 1967 on the York Minster (i.e., the Cathedral of St. Peter) in England, under attack by the death-watch beetle. "When this was completed, there was not only a solid foundation but also an organ sonata. Curious workmen had asked

11

the organist what note their drills were making as they cut into the stone for the installation of steel rods to strengthen the foundation. The organist replied, 'E-flat,' and when work was completed he played a sonata he had composed, 'The Rebirth of a Cathedral in E-flat.'"²

Perhaps someone will compose a plain song for our 165-year-old Kirkridge Farmhouse—"The Rebirth of a Farmhouse in . . . what . . . ?" A-sharp maybe! If you listen with imagination and care you may hear sounds of hammers battening windows, nailing down carpets; drills funneling insulation into walls; fireplace screens and bathroom fixtures clanging into position. What buildings in your life groan for restoration? We need to search out the key of the kingdom in which to play and pray and work towards the restoration of hearth and home, and all the shelters by which we flourish.

We who care about the rape of the land and the pollution of the air may consider together the restoration of the earth. " . . . he maketh me to lie down in green pastures, he leadeth me beside still waters, he restoreth my soul" (Psalm 23:2-3). The psalmist understood that healed nature provides healthy setting for the restoration of souls. How do we regain reverence for the earth while we exploit its resources? As we debate nuclear energy, we are reminded that plutonium, one of the most dangerous substances on earth, remains toxically active for 250,000 years, that the god of Hell is Pluto, that plutonium is thalidomide forever. Even animals do not soil their own nests. We at Kirkridge have a modest dream for restoring the earth for which we have stewardship. On Easter Sunday, April 6, 1980, we began to develop a trail, starting at the new stone chapel of Saint Columba (built by our frients of Casa Colum), passing by the Farmhouse out into the woods, up the hillside by Turning Point, and on up the mountain to the Lodge. We want to respect the land, trees, stones and creatures along "the great walk" where many pilgrims shall walk together. We want to be gentle as we open a walkway from the warm comfort of our valley to the exhilarating vistas of our mountain top. What earth belonging to your care cries out for restoration? John Cole writes, "We must begin to see the sun for its wonder as well as its warmth; for its history as well as its hydrogen.... Our solar balance needs restoring."[3] We who care about damaged lives and sin-bent history may consider together the restoration of souls. God knows the name of every person who groans in hungry death, even as our private agonies are noticed. There is no room now for chauvinism of any kind: religious (whether Christian in America, Jewish in Israel, Islamic in Iran) or national. Richard Niebuhr wrote, "We are not those who are being saved out of a perishing world but those who know the world is being saved."[4] We are restored together or not at all. Some years ago Rembrandt's painting *The Night Watch* was restored. In the process, figures which had been hidden by the dust-laden shadows of centuries appeared, astonishing everyone with newly visible design and color. Restoration of paintings and souls is revelation and transformation. Christ is the Restorer.

> Come, Lord Jesus, heal our memories. Come, Spirit, enliven our hopes. Come, Creator, restore the soul of your creation, and our souls.
>
> Amen.

Signs

And there were in the same country shepherds abiding in the field, keeping watch over their flock by night. And, lo, the angel of the Lord came upon them, and the glory of the Lord shone round about them: and they were sore afraid. And the angel said unto them, Fear not: for, behold, I bring you good tidings of great joy, which shall be to all people. For unto you is born this day in the city of David a Saviour, which is Christ the Lord. And this shall be a sign unto you; Ye shall find the babe wrapped in swaddling clothes, lying in a manger.

Luke 2:8–12 (RSV)

My young son Bob and I were walking along a road some years ago when he asked, "Dad, do you suppose anywhere in the world there is a sign that says 'trespassing'?" I asked what he meant and he said, "Well, see that sign over there that says 'no trespassing'? Is there a sign somewhere that just says 'trespassing'?" I laughed and we had fun imagining what it would be like some night to change No-signs to Yes-signs, from "no trespassing" to "trespassing," "private keep out" to "public come in," changing to "go," "parking," "safety," etc.

We human beings speak to each other in our special sign language. There is that sign outside a counselor's office: "savage breasts soothed here." And that sign on a western road: "Choose your rut carefully. You'll be in it for twenty miles." And that Texas road sign: "Smile. You're on radar." On one occasion in a Tulsa congregation, while singing "All Hail The Power of Jesus' Name," I noticed some people in the front pews using sign language, and remembered that there is a deaf ministry in that congregation. Their hands moved in a graceful sweep from shoulder to head as we sang the chorus "Crown Him. . . ." I was moved. They were turning the No of their condition into a Yes to the Lord.

One friend typically shakes hands with his arm extended, signaling to me, "this far but no further." Another responds to my "hello" by quipping his way behind a fast-talk fence which keeps me out. Anything to preclude self-revelation, vulnerability, intimacy. No-signs.

Nature speaks to us in its special sign language. In the summertime, leaves hide our view of the Appalachian ridge. But in the fall, once again we can see that massive, furrytopped ridge rolling from west to north to east, like the great arm of God coming round to hold us.

Sir Bernard Lovell writes, "We are what we know about where we came from."[1] Reminding us that when we look out into space we are looking back in time as much as 350 million years, he notes with astonishment that if in the first second after the universe burst into being ten billion years ago, "the force of attraction between protons had been only a few percent stronger, the primeval condensate would have turned into helium. No galaxies, no stars, no life would have emerged. It would have been a universe forever unknowable by living creatures."[2] To some watchers on the hillside the improbable existence of a blue-green earth and its human experiment is a yes-sign in the cosmic void.

"And this shall be a sign unto you . . ." God speaks to us in God's own special sign language—a child. Not much. A small December child. A child is birth, beginnings, seedling, potential without guarantee. A child is someone to watch. A child is the future appearing now.

God's child-sign changes the No of our condition into Yes. Are you ready to change some of your No-signs into Yes-signs?

The Word Is Very Near to You

For this Law that I enjoin on you today is not beyond your strength or beyond your reach. It is not in heaven, so that you need to wonder, "Who will go up to heaven for us and bring it down to us, so that we may hear it and keep it?" No, the Word is very near to you, it is in your mouth, and in your heart for your observance. See, today I set before you life and prosperity, death and disaster. If you obey the commandments of Yahweh your God that I enjoin on you today, if you love Yahweh your God and follow his ways, if you keep his commandments, his laws, his customs, you will love and increase, and Yahweh your God will bless you in the land which you are entering to make your own. But if your heart strays, if you refuse to listen, if you let yourself be drawn into worshipping other gods and serving them, I tell you today, you will most certainly perish; you will not live long in the land you are crossing the Jordan to enter and possess. I call heaven and earth to witness against you today: I set before you life or death, blessing or curse. Choose life, then, so that you and your descendents may live....

Deuteronomy 30:11–19 (JEB)

One morning in July, 1980, I was meditating at our family cottage in Michigan. I found myself worrying about major help which we had sought for renovating our Kirkridge buildings. If only that help came, I thought, then we could breathe easily, then we could perform our ministry properly. I began reading the Lectionary passage of the week.

"For this Law that I enjoin on you today is not beyond your strength or beyond your reach . . . No, the Word is very near to you, it is in your mouth and in your heart for your observance."

The words leapt off the page at me: "the Word is very near to you." Good news from God! "You don't have to wait for outside help. You already have assets and resources near by and within you adequate to fulfill My purposes for you." What joy to realize afresh that right now our vocation under God, at home, at work, in the nation is do-able, livable. We don't have to wait for some political, religious or financial messiah. The Kingdom of God is within our reach and strength. The Word is very near to you.

Albert Camus wrote:

> Let us not look for the door and the way out anywhere but in the wall against which we are living . . . Great ideas . . . come into the world as gently as doves. Perhaps, then, if we live attentively, we shall hear, amid the uproar of empires and nations, a faint flutter of wings, the gentle stirring of life and hope. Some will say that this hope lies in a nation; others, in a man. I believe, rather, that it is awakened, revived, nourished by millions of solitary individuals whose deeds and words every day negate frontiers and the crudest implications of history. . . . Each and every man, on the foundation of his own sufferings and joys, builds for all."[1]

The Word is as near to you as the wall against which you are now living.

The Word is not only near, but *very* near to us . . . in our mouth and in our hearts. Jesus used the term *abba* for God, an outrageously intimate term . . . "daddy," "mommy" . . . as a child would speak to a parent. We are reminded that the characteristic biblical pattern of God's self-revelation is not to the wise, rich or powerful, but to fools, the poor, children — ordinary, grass roots folk like you and me — or to the fool, the poor one, the child in us.

Abraham Heschel wrote that God in his mercy accepts even the prayers of our mouths, our lip service, taking our wooden hopes and waned faith as outer signs of an inner longing.[2] The Hebrew term *kavanah* means the inner participation of the heart. It is heart-to-heart prayer. "Sometimes, awakening on the edge of despair to weep and arising from forgetfulness, we feel how yearning moves in softly to become the lord of a restless breast, and we pass over the gap with the lightness of a dream."[3]

Over the gap of mouth-prayer into heart-prayer, *kavanah*. "Listen, listen, listen to my heart's song," whispers the yearning pray-er. The kingdom of God is within you . . . in your heart. The Word is very near to you.

During that July, my parents were celebrating their sixtieth anniversary at the family cottage. Several years ago my father lost his wedding ring there. Thorough searching failed to uncover it, so another ring was purchased. That July, my eleven-year-old stepson, Matt, was playing by the swing near the cottage. He saw something glistening on the ground. He picked it up, a gold ring, and brought it to his mother. Inside its worn surface, we read: July 14, 1920. It was my father's lost wedding ring! Matt was somewhat reluctantly persuaded to keep the secret until the anniversary celebration five days hence. My parents could scarely believe the serendipity of the lost and found ring in the sixtieth year of their marriage. All of us wondered about the marvelous synchronicity of a child at play who found such a treasure hidden underfoot in the soil of the years.

The kingdom of God is close at hand in the shining nearness of resources, institutions, relationships, selves, death, life. The Word is very near to you.

Yesterday's Will of God

The Spirit . . . drove him out into the wilderness.
Matthew 4:1 (RSV)

The wilderness image in the Bible is ambivalent, connoting deprivation, journey, transition, heightened awareness, chaotic and cleansing silence, aloneness, the presence of testing. Do you know something of what it is, with Jesus to struggle for your identity and vocation in some wilderness period of your life, a time when a fresh baptism of the Spirit has blown apart your images of self, God, life, and left you blinking in the blinding dark?

"And he was in the wilderness forty days, tempted by Satan" (Matt. 4:4).

Satan begins his questioning of Jesus each of the three times with the word *if* (Matt. 4:1–11). Should Jesus accept the traditional roles of the Messiah (to be the new Prophet, Priest, King) prescibed by his heritage and here articulated by Satan? Satan hooked into the *ifs* of Jesus.

What are your ifs or agendas from the past, laid on by your parents, peers, heritage? How is Satan hooking into your oughts and guilts to predetermine your behavior in conformity with yesterday's will of God?

Satan's function is to make tangible the tension between yesterday's will of God and today's will of God. He makes evil visible and choice unavoidable. He forces the tension between our self and our roles to the tearing point.

Jesus said *no* each time to Satan's *if*, in order to be free to say *yes* to today's will of God. How are you tempted to accept the roles, agendas, prescriptions of yesterday? What does it mean for you to say *no* to yesterday's will of God so that today's will of God for you can appear?

While being interviewed about her role in "Alice Doesn't Live

19

Here Anymore," Ellen Burstyn said, "With other characters I've had to wear a wardrobe. With Alice I could use my own skin. . . . In Strasberg's training, you learn to become strong enough to let your inner life show, which of course includes weaknesses."[1] Satan taunts us to see whether we have courage to live in our own skins where we may be apprehended by today's will of God.

"And he was with the wild beasts, and the angels ministered to him" (Matt. 4:11).

Beasts and angels gather round every cradle of holy birth, bespeaking the natural and spiritual world, and hinting of the transformation of nature and history; when the lion and lamb shall lie down together, and as comedian Woody Allen sagely notes, "the lamb shall get up!" A new earth, a new birth.

My wife, Cindy, saw a clay sculpture on the wall of an art shop. Reddish brown, round, with something white appearing out of a torn, ragged womblike opening—a child's white face. At once frivolous and ominous. Along the top of the sculpture was a number: 45970. Outside a number; inside a name. Who's got your number? Who knows your name?

That clay sculpture, reminding us that we have clay faces and feet, now hangs on the wall of our living room where we are dying to a number and living to a name; dying to a role and living to a self; *no*-ing and *yes*-ing; living in our own skin and loving the skin we're in; dying to yesterday's will of God, and living to today's will of God.

Let Your Spirit Breathe Through Me

We know that the whole creation has been groaning in travail together until now; and not only the creation, but we ourselves, who have the first fruits of the Spirit, groan inwardly as we wait for adoption as sons, the redemption of our bodies. For in this hope we were saved. Now hope that is seen is not hope. For who hopes for what he sees? But if we hope for what we do not see, we wait for it with patience.

Likewise the Spirit helps us in our weakness; for we do not know how to pray as we ought, but the Spirit himself intercedes for us with sighs too deep for words. And he who searches the hearts of men knows what is the mind of the Spirit, because the Spirit intercedes for the saints according to the will of God.

Romans 8:22–27 (RSV)

In early June you could hear the hum. Suddenly one morning it was there, rising out of the woods and swamps, ringing like an errant electric wire. A constant humming. The cicadas were back. After seventeen years! Astonishing isn't it. A seventeen-year clock. A few weeks of life, then death, seventeen years of waiting, and then new life. Cicadas.

At first the humming was gentle, comforting, reminding me of Paul's word about unceasing prayer. Maybe this was the audible prayer of God on behalf of creation, the sound of a natural choir. How beautiful! But after several days the noise began to get on my nerves, always there like a speck of dust in the eye, surrounding me, filling up every bit of silence, resonating in the sound of my own breathing. The cicadas were damaging my equanimity!

Paul wrote, "We don't know how to pray as we ought, but the Spirit helps us in our weakness . . . searching our hearts with sighs too deep for words" (Rom. 8:26). I used to sigh a lot, especially in those years when I had not yet allowed myself to cry. Sighs are tears not yet released into the world. Tears are wet sighs. It is comforting to me to think that God's Spirit is search-

21

ing, hallowing my spirit with sighs too deep for words. The sound of my own breathing is evidence of God's present invigoration of my life. Indeed, the life of the whole creation, which as Paul writes "... groans in travail ... waiting for the redemption of our bodies" (Rom. 8:22).

One day at the Nyngma Buddhist Institute in Berkeley, California, I participated in a workshop on practical mysticism. One of the meditations we did was called "The Marriage of Sound and Breath." We were instructed to center down, get into the rhythm of our own breathing, and listen. Listen to any and every sound near and far. I listened and breathed, and began to hear the screech of tires outside in the street, the movements of people in the room where I was, and then, unendingly, relentlessly the sound of a ticking nearby, a ticking that began to sound like Big Ben gonging. It was coming from a small watch on the wrist of someone a few feet from me. The sound became wedded to the rhythm of my breathing and my body-sigh became audible to me.

In recent months I have used a particular mantra in my praying. It is *Let Your Spirit Breathe Through Me.* Sometimes I inhale on the first three words and exhale on the last three. I find this practice allows me to get in touch with my body and to let my body sigh its own prayer. It seems to cleanse and clarify me, and tune me into the sound of my own sighing, perhaps even the sound of the Spirit sighing within me. If some prayers are prayers of *intention*, this prayer is one of *attention*. Occasionally, as my mood or condition or that of the world suggests, I will use a different verb—"blow"..."burn"..."shine"..."sing"...etc. This versatility of verbal image releases the variety of yearnings and needs moving in me. Often I will let the last word of the mantra be the name of someone special to me, or some person/event in the world: Let Your Spirit Breathe Through ... Barbara ... Kirkridge ... the Polish people. Petition interweaves with intercession. So we can participate in God's prayer for the whole creation straining towards the redemption of our bodies, and the mystical body of all creation.

Ho—ping

May he enlighten the eyes of your mind so that you can see what hope his call holds for you. . . .

Ephesians 1:18 (JEB)

Recently on the Op-Ed page of the *New York Times*, in the space often filled by a Mobil Oil ad, I saw a public service ad about *The Cornucopia Project*. It was an invitation from Rodale Press in Emmaus, Pennsylvania to become knowledgeable about rising food costs and involved in working for constructive changes in the U.S. food system. I visited the Rodale people, and discovered a book by Medard Gabel: *Ho—ping: Food for Everyone* (Doubleday). Gabel, Director of *The Cornucopia Project*, also works with Buckminster Fuller developing World games as an alternative to War games. He notes that *ho—ping* is the Chinese word for peace, whose literal translation means "food for every one."

Can anything good come out of Emmaus? You bet! The Rodale people are hopers, and I'm glad I stumbled upon them because I can use some hope right now. How can I be hopeful when, these days, tobacco farmers are being promised higher subsidies at the same time the government program to help people stop smoking is being threatened and cutbacks mandated for food stamps for the poor? How can I be hopeful when right-wing dictatorships in Latin and South America are being assured that human rights will now be de-emphasized in favor of military security and economic stability, while thousands of priests, nuns, editors, peasants and workers for agrarian reform are being tortured and murdered with the connivance of those governments? How can I be hopeful when some of my friends suffer with cancer, and the powers of death grin at me from within and without? Hoping encourages me to say Yes to those things in myself and society that affirm life, and No to those things that affirm death.

Hoping is an ethics of liberation, a vocation to work on the small transformations feasible in our own lives and systems. Heroic life style changes, important as they are to our own integrity and economy, cannot solve global problems. Our institutions and governments must also be transformed. We at Kirkridge are learning how to do more with less. We sold our stationwagon and use our own cars to make airport pickups and food purchases. We have redesigned office space to provide necessary functions at less heating cost while freeing much of the former office space for other uses. We are inviting people to bring their own linens/towels: this benefits them by allowing us to maintain current prices instead of raising them; and it benefits us by cutting laundry expense and large scale use of our limited water supply. We are serving tasty and more nutritious meals without red meat and without raising prices, using cookbooks such as *More With Less* by Doris Longacre, Herald Press, Scottsdale, Pennsylvania. It's surprising and exciting to discover how many ways we can do more with less. Richard Barnet reminds us in *The Lean Years* that the five critical resource systems in the world: food, water, human energy, nonhuman energy, non-fuel minerals are interconnected.[1] These resource systems are all too important to leave to private interests alone. There must come some form of public control of oil, water, food, etc. How are you working on the small transformations feasible in your own life and scene?

Hoping is an ethics of resistance, a vocation to dig in our Gospel heels in the face of injustice at work, in the community and nation. In a darkening time, if we cannot change things, we can refuse to be changed by things. We can refuse to be swept or seduced away from our own anchorage. If we cannot reverse the arms race we can resist it patiently and passionately. If we cannot overcome, we can refuse to be overcome. If we cannot transform, we can refuse to be conformed. We can resurrect gospel terms like endurance and withstanding. Hope deepens into eschatology, effectiveness into fidelity. None of us knows when or whether a seed of courage will sprout out of dark ground, nor when a leaven of truth will permeate the lump of falsity. We do know we are called in hope to keep scattering seeds and sneaking in the leaven. The Sabbath was a survival institution for Jews through centuries of persecution, enabling them to remember, and so to hope. What are our survival structures of memory and hope today, where our vocation and identity are celebrated and energized? What do we resist in this culture and who are our fellow resistors? What boundaries will we refuse to cross? What evils will break our silence?

Safety and Vulnerability

Yahweh Sabaoth, bring us back, let your face smile on us and we shall be safe.

Psalm 80:3 (JEB)

Come, let us praise Yahweh joyfully, acclaiming the Rock of our safety.

Psalm 95:1 (JEB)

There is a time to leave home, and a time to come home:
a time to hide, and a time to come out of hiding
a time to advance, and a time to retreat
a time to make it happen, and a time to let it happen
a time to ask questions, and a time to find answers
a time to be safe, and a time to be vulnerable.

Vulnerability exposes us to the ache throbbing in the heart of the world and in our own hearts. It keeps us engaged, invested, hurting and therefore hoping. It keeps us from cold detachment or uncaring cynicism. Self-mockery provides distance for our aching, a sense of history and of humor. It protects us against self-pity, sentimentality, and taking ourselves and our causes too seriously.

To be vulnerable is to suffer loss, to have to learn how to grieve. To be vulnerable is to have our own judgmental spirit broken again and again by the acknowledgment of our own failures and betrayals. It is to lose immunity against the cries, laughs and songs of others. When we bcome vulnerable, we are accessible to be known. We receive the gift of self-revelation which is the gift of intimacy, which is the sharing of privacies. To be human is to be vulnerable. But to be constantly, totally vulnerable is to be dehumanized. Survival requires safety . . . sometimes.

Every person has safety needs. Remember that gospel hymn — "Leaning on the everlasting arms . . . safe and secure from all alarms?" Until I grew up and came to know my own need for safety, I associated that hymn with weakness and a need for otherworldly crutches. I know now that there is a time for sanctuary, oasis, shelter. There is a time for licking wounds, restoring the soul, waiting for strength to be renewed. If in Jungian terms the masculine God calls us out of our safety to leave home, the feminine God calls us out of our vulnerability to come home. And blessed are those who have ears to hear their calling.

In Elie Wiesel's drama *The Madness of God*, the interrogator asks the old rabbi, "What is prayer? Is it question or is it answer?" The Rabbi replies, "It is both. If you have questions, prayer leads to answers. If you have answers, prayer brings questions." The questioner and answer-giver are one. The rock of our safety lodges in the rapids of our vulnerability. As, one by one, doctrines, visions, strategies, persons, institutions demonstrate their fallibility and mortality . . . wherein does our safety lie?

For me, safety lies in the trust that nothing in life or death can separate me from the love of God manifest in Christ. There is a time to be safe and a time to be vulnerable. And blessed are those who know the timing of their time.

Do You Want To Be Healed?

> Now there is in Jerusalem . . . a pool . . . which has five porticoes. In these lay a multitude of invalids, blind, lame, paralyzed. One man was there who had been ill for thirty-eight years.
>
> *John 5:2-5* (RSV)

In the summer of 1965 I was studying the Gospel of John with a Mission Group developing a medical ministry in a Philadelphia ghetto. The week of my thirty-eighth birthday we explored this story of the paralytic, and I heard the Gospel addressed to me in the first person singular. How was *I* in-valid, crippled, paralyzed? I began to understand that I was crippled in my capacity for intimacy, that I was unable to reveal myself to one other person. So, I kept a sincere, frozen smile on my pastoral face. How about you? In what way have you been in-valid, crippled for 18 or 38 or 58 years? A woman spoke of her in-validity as an inner experience of impotence, the sapping of her will so that she was unable decisively to say Yes or No, to set limits, to decide. How about you?

"When Jesus saw him and knew that he had been lying there a long time, he said to him, 'Do you want to be healed?'" (John 5:6).

Is there anybody in your life now who sees you and knows you? A cry from the edge of being: "I wish someone could see me, really see me, see my pain as well as my confidence, see my terror as well as my composure." Another cry: "There is no one within fifty miles of where I live with whom I can share my deepest pain or joy." Can you imagine being seen and known by God? Do you want to be healed? What a question! Cruel, callous? Or, penetrating, caring to the core of the man's being? I used to believe that God was in my oughts ninety-five percent of the time and in my wants almost never. I learned to distrust my inmost yearnings and to over-value the agendas and expectations laid on me by parents, church, society. But Jesus tunes into our want-energies. If you take a moment and make an I WANT list, what pours out of your insides?

Do you want to be healed? Health. Health is a matter of wholeness and not perfection. Health does not have to do with striving to be better or not to make mistakes. Health has to do with being real and offering our sins, mistakes and brokenness as multicolored threads to be woven into a rich tapestry of humanity by the healing grace of God. Health is the integration of erotic and spiritual energy, congruence of the mystical and the political, the integrity of our being and doing. "Evil . . .is the part trying to be the whole; healing is the whole overcoming the part."[1] "God sends the wound; God is the wound; God is wounded; God heals the wound."[2]

Do you want to be healed?

"The sick man answered him, 'Sir, I have no man to put me into the pool when the water is troubled, and while I am going down another steps before me'" (John 5:7).

In our in-validity we make excuses and say, "I can't." We assume a victim mentality and refuse to acknowledge our participation in our paralysis.

Some doctors today encourage cancer patients not to be victims but agents and to say, "I am cancering." We too need to acknowledge that we participate in our paralysis and can and must participate in our healing. Victims milk their disabilities and manipulate others into perpetuating a dependent-paternal relationship. Agents own the traps they choose to stay in, or the action that leads to their liberation. A man wrote me, "Your open expression of your affection for me is healing, for few people have done that. Or perhaps I have been unable to perceive it or receive it." Do you feel that you are unable or unwilling to receive the love of another, even of God? Could you unlock your heart a little? Do you want to be healed?

"Jesus said to him, 'Rise, take up your pallet, and walk.' At

once the man was healed, and he took up his pallet and walked"
(John 5:8-9).

Jesus did not deal with the in-valid man as though he were a
victim: he didn't offer him a crutch or a helping hand or money.
Jesus engaged him as an agent and told him to get up off his . . .
pallet and walk! Cruel, unfeeling? No! Deeply respectful of our
human capacity, even in our in-validity, to take responsibility
for our lives and participate in our own healing. No one can
help a chick out of an eggshell or open a rose or give another
wholeness. The God who sees and knows us in our crippled condition invites us with deep affection and respect to release our
powerful want-energies, to rise up with "healing in our wings"
and to participate in a healing community. As Morton Kelsey
has said, "My meditation is never completed until someone feels
more loved by me."   Do you want to be healed?

Christmas Is Crossing Over

> So do not be surprised, my brothers, if the people of the world hate you. We know that we have left death and crossed over into life; we know it because we love our brothers.... Our love should not be just words and talk; it must be true love, which shows itself in action.
>
> *I John 3:13,14,18* (RSV)

On September 9, 1980 at 6:50 A.M. eight persons, including Daniel and Phillip Berrigan, slipped by guards into the General Electric plant in King of Prussia, Pennsylvania. (This plant makes the Mark 12A first strike re-entry vehicle, intended for Minuteman III and Trident II. One warhead can produce ninety Hiroshimas.) The eight took hammers and beat on the missile cone heads, literally trying to "beat swords into plowshares." The action involved <u>minor</u> damage as a way of dramatizing the <u>major</u> human damage being readied by the war machine today. The action was in the tradition of Jesus who also did minor property damage when he overturned the Temple tables as a way of dramatizing the major human damage being perpetrated by the Temple system of the time. Jesus paid for that action with his life.

The Plowshares Eight may pay for their witness with several years of their lives, in prison. On October 20, 1980 I visited five of the men being held in the Montgomery County jail in Norristown, Pennsylvania. Dressed in prison blue, they spoke of Bible study daily, opportunities to help other prisoners in legal and personal ways, spiritual preparations for trial, sentencing and years in prison. Their faces radiated a quiet joy.

Later that fall Daniel Berrigan, out on bail for medical reasons, led a retreat at Kirkridge on the theme *Election and Vocation.* Insights abounded: "The Christian Gospel is indictable by the State.... If Christ, not America, tells us who we are, where we come from and where we are to go, we are anarchic to the

State. . . . Salvation is found today by most people in the State. . . . The bomb is our security, our savior, our salvation. . . . In order to 'protect' our security we will do literally anything the State tells us to do—including killing hundreds of millions of human beings and possibly destroying the earth. . . . Yet, Christians are called to *give* life rather than *take* it. . . . We cannot follow Christ today without losing something, without danger or sacrifice. . . . People find it more sane to contemplate nuclear suicide than civil disobedience. . . . We are held back by fear of consequences, but once the inner fear is conquered, the consequences are quite bearable. . . ."

Where shall we look for the coming of Christ at Christmas? A TV reporter, commenting on the delight at the Pentagon with additional billions going to defense (offense?) said, "It's like Christmas at the Pentagon!" Is it? In Salt Lake City, a group of church people, including Mormons, began a vigil in early 1981 in protest against the MX shell game planned for their state. Some of them did not believe it is God's will that their holy land should become so desecrated, only the will of the American government. Shall we look for Christ wherever ordinary people vigil, walk, banner, leaflet for peace? The Christian Church is the only voluntary institution, located at every corner of city and town in America, which could mount a peace witness to say "No" to nuclear war and "Yes" to nuclear disarmament. If each of us makes peace witness where we live and work we can become a leaven of hope. Could Christ come in you and me at Christmas?

Perhaps we could see Christ coming in the grey, fortress-like jail in Norristown, Pennsylvania. Christmas is crossing over. God crossed over to us in Christ, and every time we cross over to God's kingdom of peace, Christ comes again and Christmas happens. John Schuchardt, one of the Plowshares Eight, a lawyer, wrote from his prison cell:

> If there is one word to describe our preparations for our action, our ten hours in the holding cells following arrest, our appear-

ances in court, our lives in prison, it is JOY. This too describes the feeling of our communities and friends; each day brings new brightness: cards and letters filled with color, flowers, doves of peace, ocean waves, waterfalls, trees of life. . . . Many of these greetings hang on our cell walls. . . . We know that all of this is a gift; only God can bring joy and true happiness to a prison cell. The Old Testament prophets and Jesus point to strange paradoxes: joy in suffering; sacrifice and resistance as the *only* alternative to complicity in the crimes of the state. Spiritual death is the refusal to believe that peace is possible. . . . Love leads us into the way of peacemaking even though we are full of fear, doubt and uncertainty. In this moment we somehow crossed over. Cross over too. Cross over now. Brothers and sisters, we greet you all with love.

Christmas is crossing over from fear to love, from serving the bomb to serving God. Whenever we cross over, Christmas happens, Christ is born in us. Any day can be Christmas Day, even today. Sisters and brothers, let's cross over together.

The Art of Leaving

I have said all this to you to keep you from falling away. They will put you out of the synagogues; indeed, the hour is coming when whoever kills you will think he is offering service to God. And they will do this because they have not known the Father, nor me. But I have said these things to you, that when their hour comes you may remember that I told you of them.

I did not say these things to you from the beginning, because I was with you. But now I am going to him who sent me; yet none of you asks me, "Where are you going?" But because I have said these things to you, sorrow has filled your hearts. Nevertheless I tell you the truth: it is to your advantage that I go away, for if I do not go away, the Counselor will not come to you; but if I go, I will send him to you.

John 16:1–7 (RSV)

Henri Nouwen suggests that we need to cultivate "the art of leaving . . . the ability to be articulately absent . . . creative withdrawal."[1]

The art of leaving: to allow space for another to expand, develop, be. Nouwen continues: "Physical presence not only invites but also blocks intimate communication. In our preresurrection state our bodies hide as much as they reveal."[2] We need to grow into a "maturing interplay between absence and presence" in creating a style of parenting, spousing and befriending which encourages the autonomy of the other. Alan Paton writes of thus leaving his adolescent son:

> Go forward, eager . . . child, see here I begin to take my hands away from you, I shall see you walk careless on the edges of the precipice, but if you wish you shall hear no words come out of me; my whole soul will be sick with apprehension, but I shall not disobey you. . . . Go forward, go forward, I hold the bandages and ointments ready. . . .[3]

If we do not program our children for repetition, but encourage them towards self-discovery, we shall know the pain and promise of leaving them and allowing them to leave.

The art of leaving: to allow space for one's self to center, deepen, be. Twelve families living in an apartment building in Boston call their intentional community *Commonplace*. They have developed, in the intensity and proximity of their living together, a way of letting each other know when they need to be left alone for the moment—in the code phrase, "It's not a good time." When I allow my solitude time/space to be impinged upon or eroded, hostility grows in me to the point that I need to leave. My capacity to be available for another depends upon my ability to protect my privacy.

The art of leaving: to clarify who's responsible for what. Some time ago I experienced the Tavistock model of leadership—a cool system in which leaders stay "in role," observe precise time boundaries, and establish distance between themselves and group participants by impassive face and behavior. It requires participants to take responsibility for creating their own community. Most religious systems are warm, stressing the self-giving of leaders and seducing participants into a dependent acceptance of community created for them. Perhaps we could be cooled off a bit, moving away from a paternal-maternal style, to that embodied by Jesus when he told the paralytic to pick up his own bed and walk (John 5:2-8).

The art of leaving: to assess availability/indispensability. When a friend of mine got close to vacation each summer, he would begin to joke about leaving, not being missed, indeed not having a job when he returned. His identity trembled towards non-being when he stopped working. Many of us are willing to be constantly available so as to be able to keep on hugging the myth of our indispensability. Yet we know in our heads that when we leave a place, role or relationship—temporarily or permanently—people rapidly learn to get along very well without us. When we face the fear of not being needed, it can be quite a relief to discover that we are not indispensable to any one but God.

The art of leaving: God's way. In one of his last conversations with his friends, Jesus said to them, "It is to your advantage that I go away, for if I do not go away, the Counselor will not come to you." By a creative withdrawal of himself, Jesus allowed the Spirit to abide in us always and everywhere as comforter, guide and leader. God trusts us enough to leave us alone in this world, in the Spirit.

Go Up Into The Gaps

The word of the Lord came to me: "Son of man, prophesy against the prophets of Israel, prophesy and say to those who prophesy out of their own minds: 'Hear the word of the Lord!' Thus says the Lord God, Woe to the foolish prophets who follow their own spirit, and have seen nothing! Your prophets have been like foxes among ruins, O Israel. You have not gone up onto the breaches, or built up a wall for the house of Israel, that it might stand in battle in the day of the Lord. They have spoken falsehood and divined a lie; they say, 'Says the Lord,' when the Lord has not sent them, and yet they expect Him to fulfil their word. Have you not seen a delusive vision, and uttered a lying divination, whenever you have said, 'Says the Lord,' although I have not spoken?"

Ezekiel 13:1–7 (RSV)

Annie Dillard writes:

Ezekiel excoriates false prophets as those who have "not gone up into the gaps." The gaps are the thing. The gaps are the spirit's own home, the altitudes and latitudes so dazzlingly spare and clean that the spirit can discover itself for the first time like a once-blind man unbound. The gaps are clefts in the rock where you cower to see the back parts of God; they are the fissures between mountains, and cells the wind lances through, the icy narrowing fiords splitting the cliffs of mystery. Go up into the gaps.[1]

We remember that the word *spirit* in the Greek is neuter, in Hebrew is feminine, and only in the Christian era has it by custom been masculinized. The Spirit is at home in the gaps of our land and lives. Wind and water are Her elements. She waits for us in the gaps. Go up into the gaps.

Kirkridge is perched on a hill between Wind Gap to the west and Water Gap to the east. Sometimes we hear the Spirit beating at our windowpanes, watch the trees bending and know that

37

our life structures are fragile before the furious blast. When the breeze has gentled upon us, all may be clear and clean. Sometimes we see the melting snow become a torrent roaring down the mountainside and know that our secure order can be swept away by the tears of many years. When the grieving is done, the stream can carry our yearnings toward a quiet valley.

Go up into the gaps of broken dreams, failed promises, the limits of a longed for intimacy, the unredeemed parts of ourselves and the intractable cruelties of our society. Go up and stand and look. We must still discern the spirits. Ezekiel says, "Woe to the foolish prophets who follow their own spirit and have seen nothing!. . . like foxes among ruins." Kirkridge is on Fox Gap Road. Even here, especially here, we must beware of being foolish prophets who have seen nothing and yet say, "Thus says the Lord." If we have not seen anything, we must be quiet. A silent witness is better than a deceived or deceiving witness.

But the witness is the thing. The witness of going up into the gaps and standing and waiting and enduring. We try to close the gaps, bandage wounds, resolve conflict and reconcile opposites. But aloneness abides even in community. Nor does God fill the gaps. Bonhoeffer writes from prison, separated from his loved ones, "It is nonsense to say that God fills the gap; he does not fill it, but keeps it empty so that our communion with another may be kept alive, even at the cost of pain. . . ."[2] If we follow our pain it will lead us towards tomorrow.

Gaps are breaches in our defenses against love . . . openings of vulnerability and potentiality. Gaps are questions to be lived, wounds which are occasions of new creation. Where there is a gap, all things are possible.

The Spirit is at home in the gaps of our land and lives. Water and wind are Her elements. She waits for us in the gaps. Go up into the gaps.

Investing in God's Future

Jeremiah said, "The word of the Lord came to me: Behold, Hanamel the son of Shallum your uncle will come to you and say, 'Buy my field which is at Anathoth, for the right of redemption by purchase is yours.' Then Hanamel my cousin came to me in the court of the guard, in accordance with the word of the Lord, and said to me, 'Buy my field which is at Anathoth in the land of Benjamin for the right of possession and redemption is yours; buy it for yourself.' Then I knew that this was the word of the Lord.

"And I bought the field at Anathoth from Hanamel my cousin, and weighed out the money to him, seventeen shekels of silver. I signed the deed, sealed it, got witnesses, and weighed the money on scales. Then I took the sealed deed of purchase, containing the terms and conditions, and the open copy; and I gave the deed of purchase to Baruch the son of Neriah, son of Mahseiah, in the presence of Hanamel my cousin, in the presence of the witnesses who signed the deed of purchase, and in the presence of all the Jews who were sitting in the court of the guard. I charged Baruch in their presence, saying, 'Thus says the Lord of hosts, the God of Israel: Take these deeds, both this sealed deed of purchase and this open deed, and put them in an earthenware vessel, that they may last for a long time. For thus says the Lord of hosts, the God of Israel: Houses and fields and vineyards shall again be bought in this land.'"

Jeremiah 32:6-15 (RSV)

In 588 B.C., when Jerusalem was under Babylonian siege and Jeremiah was in prison, Jeremiah bought a field in his hometown of Anathoth, only two miles from the besieged capital. It was a vivid demonstration of his faith that, despite the desperate circumstances, God had a future for that land and Jeremiah would have a part in it. When others were selling out, giving up, or hunkering down, Jeremiah was investing in God's future.

God's people in any time are those—inside or outside the Church—who risk their resources and lives in the darkest of times to invest in God's future.

God's people are those who believe that God is working out the divine purpose in this world, that God will keep the rainbow promise to Noah not to destroy the earth, and that this promise can be trusted.

What does God's future look like, sound like? How can we recognize that future in process? God's future is breaking in wherever there is evidence of human transformation, whenever energy yields movement towards wholeness and reconciliation and health. The *shalom* of God is God's future rising up in this world, though tiny and hidden like a seed germinating in the earth night and day, growing toward visible birth with the inevitability of the power of the universe behind it.

Two men bought a rundown farmhouse in northeastern Pennsylvania some years ago. They had been renovating that old house and developing a garden out of the dank swampland. A stonemason taught them how to build with stone, and one summer they worked with him and a few friends to build a sixteen-foot-diameter chapel, with walls two feet thick of stone gathered from their land.

The architect told them, "It will still be here in 500 years," long after other buildings around and all our bodies will be gone. Foolish? Maybe. Who knows? God knows. It is now a center for growing numbers of people who come to rest and pray in it. It is a healing space. It gathers the spirits of Spirit-blessed people. It is becoming a modest holy place. The Kingdom of God is like two men who built a chapel. . . .

Two years ago a woman was divorced. For weeks she cried and dwelt in lonely sorrow. Then, like the paralytic in Jesus' story, she decided she wanted to be healed. So she went to a retreat for formerly married people, found others on a similar journey, comfort that she wasn't alone, and courage to pick up her life and walk with it into a new future: God's future.

Back in her midwestern hometown, she and others formed a support group for divorced and separated persons. She writes, "I am a tent dweller who can no longer be devastated as I once was when my first house was destroyed. I let go of yesterday's fears and embrace today's hopes!" That woman is living into tomorrow's will of God, believing also that God will participate passionately in that future.

In April 1980 three women and four men stood together in silence outside the river entrance of the Pentagon. One of them held a homemade poster. Passersby paused to look. There were snapshots of nine children. "Beautiful kids," some said. Others looked, nodded, and turned away. Above the nine pictures were the words: "We Want a Future for Our Children." Below the nine pictures were the words: "And Yours."

A little band of seven people protesting the nuclear arms race in the face of the world's most powerful and deadly war machine. Hopeless? Ridiculous? Maybe. Who knows? God knows. Despite the powers of death outside us and inside us, we can lift a tiny banner of peace. While trying not to be damn fools, we can be willing fools for Christ's sake.

Sometimes we long to invest in God's future but are fearful of jeopardizing our own present. We may feel trapped, unable to find a safe way into that future. We anguish in the middle of nowhere. A middle-aged scientist writes, "By all contemporary American standards I have succeeded beyond most people's wildest dreams (wonderful wife, high-paying job, large house, children). I am a modern-day rich young ruler! I see the path that I should take, working full time on hunger and peace programs, using my scientific training to help bring us one small step closer to social justice for all peoples of this small planet. But I can't let go; I can't find a suitable avenue to make what I see as the necessary changes." (Read: "I won't take the risk of giving up all I have to follow Christ without a clear view of what's ahead!")

We are like that man, wanting to invest in God's future but afraid to let go of a safe and secure present. He is honestly struggling and searching. I believe the ferment of the Spirit is sighing within him to bring forth God's future—perhaps pain-filled but surely also joy-filled—like the anguish and joy of birth.

Sometimes the trap is external, sometimes internal. All of us live in closets where some parts of our authentic lives and selves cannot be shared. To some degree all of us suffer the anguish of having to please other people by denying some of our own inner reality. We long to be congruent, to be able to express power-fully and warmly in our outer lives and relationships all the pas-sion and yearning energy moving within us. We long to bring our "oughts" and our "wants" in focus.

We long to be honest with ourselves, with others, and with God. The time and timing of our coming out or going back or leaving home or picking up our life and walking with it, must be our own. But God's future awaits our choosing to be real.

William Stringfellow said, "Resurrection talk is facetious un-til the power of death is understood and lived through: Resur-rection should mean involvement in the life of this world on terms that always mean risking death in some form."[1]

The middle-aged scientist risks death in the form of letting some measure of material security go in order to begin an uncer-tain vocation. Those seven people risk being ridiculed and dis-missed in their efforts to confront power with truth. The di-vorced woman risks the burden of becoming involved in the pain of others. The chapel builders risk putting all they have in-to a little venture whose future they cannot foretell or guaran-tee, and which will return to them nothing except the gratitude of those who are touched by God within its walls. What risks are you willing to consider taking as you struggle to invest in God's future?

Do You Remember Me?

And Mary said,
"My soul magnifies the Lord,
and my spirit rejoices in God my Saviour,
for he has regarded the low estate of his
handmaiden.
For behold, henceforth all generations
will call me blessed;
for he who is mighty has done great
things for me,
and holy is his name.
And his mercy is on those who fear him
from generation to generation.
He has shown strength with his arm,
He has scattered the proud in the
imagination of their hearts,
He has put down the mighty from their
thrones,
and exalted those of low degree;
He has filled the hungry with good
things,
and the rich he has sent empty away.
He has helped his servant Israel,
in remembrance of his mercy,
as he spoke to our fathers,
to Abraham and to his posterity for
ever.'"

Luke 1:46–55 (RSV)

Those are poignant words: ". . . He has remembered me, his lowly servant." Unimportant, unworthy me! I can surely identify with that, can't you? How could God remember me? Small potatoes, me! Lousy Christian, me! I think even the most self-confident of us has moments when, for whatever reason, inside he or she feels unimportant, unworthy.

Recently, I saw an "important man" whom I had met briefly

43

on several occasions. Once I even had a half-hour conversation with this man, and so I had every reason to believe that he would know me by sight and by name. Yet, on this occasion, whether I was awed by his position or what, I found myself afraid that he wouldn't remember me. So, I avoided the pain of the possibility of his not remembering me by hurrying over to say, "Hello, I'm Bob Raines!" before he could get that blank look on his face which puts the skids to our egos. Our human cry to each other and to God is "Do you remember me?"

The sun is so large that if it were hollow it could contain more than one million worlds the size of our earth. There are stars in space so large that they could easily hold five-hundred million suns the size of ours. There are about a hundred-billion stars in the average galaxy and at least a hundred-million galaxies in known space. The God of all that remembers me?

Yet, the last words of that thief on the cross next to Jesus were, "Remember me when you come into your Kingdom." And Jesus promised that he would. Can you feel even a little bit of the unbelievable joy of that promise? The Gospel is the good news that God *does* remember you and me, day by day.

In the early 1970s, First Community Church in Columbus, Ohio was engaged in a prison ministry. Prisoners from the Ohio Penitentiary were sometimes allowed to participate in study groups, social activities and worship on Sunday morning. It was something to see the church parking lot full of late model cars with a huge old, orange bus in the middle, a bus with the words "Ohio State Penitentiary." A few church members were upset about the potential dangers of getting involved with convicts. They asked us to stop the ministry. A church debate began. Shortly after, a letter came to me from a stranger:

> Dear Rev. Raines, Our family lives on Lincoln Road behind your church so I guess that you could say we are neighbors. We are members of Our Lady of Victory parish. We have been aware of the activity on the part of those people from FCC who are concerned about and involved in rehabilitating prisoners. Perhaps it would be of some comfort to you to know that you

have neighbors who approve and support the efforts of your groups to help these men. We live in the neighborhood and we are just as concerned about the safety of our children as any parents, but we believe that what you are doing will, in the end, bring about the kind of world we want for our children and further God's Kingdom which we believe is why we are all here together. We will keep you and yours in our prayers.

God was remembering all of us through that letter from one of our Catholic neighbors.

Our prison ministry was seeking to embody in a tiny and temporary way the promise that Jesus made 2,000 years ago to that thief convict who asked to be remembered.

Is it presumptuous of us to think that God wants us to remember him? I don't think so. Remember Jesus' words to his friends at the Last Supper: "Do this in remembrance of me." Don't forget me. Remember me. Remember me in this way as you gather together. Whenever we worship, or pray, or love, we are remembering God from the heart.

We remember God when we remember each other, when we reach out to touch someone who used to be close to us but now has become distant and strange, emotionally remote. Hannah Green writes affectionately about her great-grandmother, "She was very loving, and one time when she was very old and her memory had begun to fail, she came up to Grandpa Nye at a garden party and put her old hands around her son's face. 'I don't know who you are,' she said, 'but I know that you are someone that I love very much.'"

Is there someone whom you might remember, as though to say: "I'm not quite sure who you are anymore, but I know that I love you very much." It takes courage to do that and a longing to be close again.

I was in New Haven, Connecticut not long ago, in the Yale Divinity School Refectory, and happened to see a man sitting at a table by himself. It was Roland Bainton, one of my teachers over thirty years ago, now retired. I went over to sit with him. He had lost his wife six years ago, he told me. He began to talk about his life. A waitress came by, put a saucer on the table and said, "Here's your applesauce," and he said, "Oh, thank you for remembering." He told me that he always takes applesauce when he comes through the line. He eats there because he is alone. That day there didn't happen to be any applesauce — or he didn't see any while he was going through the line — and so he didn't get any. This waitress must have noticed over the months, or years, that he always took applesauce. She saw that he didn't have any that day and so she brought some to him. She noticed him and remembered him.

Is there someone in the routine of your job, at home, or in the city somewhere — someone lost in some institution of the city, prison, nursing home, mental hospital, whatever — someone that you might remember with a little applesauce gift of love?

Dragons and Princesses

And Jacob was left alone; and a man wrestled with him until the breaking of the day.

Genesis 32:24 (RSV)

One night several years ago, I was sitting at a table with members of my sharing group in Bethel, Maine. In the sparring conversation a sore spot was touched in me. An ache started moving. I knew I was going to cry. I hadn't cried for years, maybe decades. I resisted; my neck muscles distended until my chin hit the table and the tears of forty years poured out. The heaving hurts of all my life shook loose the tight identities of person and profession. The frail structures of my inner and outer being were overwhelmed. I went out into the night alone, groping among my multiple selves.

Do you know what it is to be mugged by some awful power in the night? Sometimes an inner ache breaks the bonds of polite control and leaves us quivering with questions. Sometimes external events destroy our neat/obsolete design in the sky and leave us shivering with fearful fantasies.

> When the man saw that he did not prevail against Jacob, he touched the hollow of his thigh and Jacob's thigh was put out of joint as he wrestled with him. Then he said, "Let me go, for the day is breaking." But Jacob said, "I will not let you go, unless you bless me." And he said to him, "What is your name?" And he said "Jacob." Then he said, "Your name shall no more be called Jacob, but Israel, for you have striven with God and with men and have prevailed." . . . And there he blessed him.
>
> *Gen. 32:25–29 (RSV)*

As a child I learned to deny my demons in the dark, repress my negative feelings, hold in my tears, muffle my passion, and cover my anger. Surface harmony at the cost of emotional honesty. Premature turning of the other cheek. Letting the demon go without a blessing. Since Bethel, I have been learning that the way to drain my demons of their destructivity is to wrestle them to a blessing, to refuse to let them go until they yield me their creative energy.

The demon in the dark is the voice of generative energy within us speaking through dreams or conscious meditation, breaking through our anger and ecstasy, pouring out in every tear. When we have courage to identify with that which haunts us, to embrace the inner stranger, we are transformed. When I can admit my fears to another person who honors them and holds them for me to see, they become even friendly, like Maurice Sendak's *Wild Things* or Max Ernst's *Dark Forests*.

Sometimes my demons turn into angels before my eyes. The poet Rilke asks, "How should we be able to forget those ancient myths that are at the beginning of all peoples, the myths about dragons that at the last moment turn into princesses; perhaps the dragons of our lives are princesses who are only waiting to see us once beautiful and brave."[1] Our dragons . . . princesses? Our demons . . . angels? Our assailant . . . God?

"So Jacob called the name of the place Peniel, saying 'For I have seen God face to face, and yet my life is preserved.' The sun rose upon him as he passed . . . limping" (Gen. 32:30–31).

Jacob was named and lamed. You and I will be given a new name, a new identity, if we struggle to the dawn-death, and a scar to remember it by. No naming without a laming. God scars those he names with some mark of meaning, some thorn in the flesh which we bear in our bodies all our days to remind us we have seen God face to face.

What is your name?

Where are you lame?

Are you limping in the daylight?

Go and Touch

Ahab told Jezebel all that Elijah had done, and how he had slain all the prophets with the sword. Then Jezebel sent a messenger to Elijah, saying, "So may the gods do to me, and more also, if I do not make your life as the life of one of them by this time tomorrow." Then he was afraid, and he arose and went for his life, and came to Beer-sheba, which belongs to Judah, and left his servant there.

But he himself went a day's journey into the wilderness, and came and sat down under a broom tree; and he asked that he might die saying, "It is enough; now O Lord, take away my life; for I am no better than my fathers." And he lay down and slept under a broom tree; and behold, an angel touched him, and said to him, "Arise and eat." And he looked, and behold there was at his head a cake baked on hot stones and a jar of water. And he ate and drank, and lay down again. And the angel of the Lord came again a second time, and touched him, and said, "Arise and eat, else the journey will be too great for you." And he arose, and ate and drank, and went in the strength of that food forty days and forty nights to Horeb the mount of God.

And there he came to a cave, and lodged there; and behold, the word of the Lord came to him, and he said to him, "What are you doing here, Elijah?" He said, "I have been very jealous for the Lord, the God of hosts; for the people of Israel have forsaken thy covenant, thrown down thy altars, and slain thy prophets with the sword; and I, even I only, am left; and they seek my life, to take it away." And he said, "Go forth, and stand upon the mount before the Lord." And behold, the Lord passed by, and a great and strong wind rent the mountains, and broke in pieces the rocks before the Lord, but the Lord was not in the wind; and after the wind an earthquake, but the Lord was not in the earthquake; and after the earthquake a fire, but the Lord was not in the fire; and after the fire a still small voice. And when Elijah heard it, he wrapped his face in his mantle and went out and stood at the entrance of the cave. And behold, there came a voice to him, and said, "What are you doing here, Elijah?" He said, I have been very jealous for the Lord, the God of hosts; for the people of Israel have forsaken thy covenant, thrown down thy altars and slain thy prophets with the sword; and I, even I only, am left; and they seek my life, to take it away." And the Lord said to him, "Go, return on your way to the wilderness of Damascus; and when you arrive, you shall anoint Hazael to be king over Syria; and Jehu the son of Nimshi you shall anoint to be king over Israel; and Elisha the son of Shaphat of Abelmeholah you shall anoint to be prophet in your place."

1 Kings 19:1–16 (RSV)

We saw the over-turned car on Route 191 going down the mountain at 9:05 P.M. that September night. On hands and knees we pulled open the front door, and two young men crawled out. One, bleeding, sobbing, shaking, cried out loud, "What am I doing here?" We put a jacket on him, rubbed his shoulders, touched the cut on his face. Neither of the two men was seriously injured. Other cars stopped, and we all waited with them until help came.

Elijah, fleeing from the wrath of Jezebel, fell asleep on his journey. He was wakened by the touch of an angel and discovered food and water at his head. He ate and drank, and in the strength of that nourishment came to the mountain of God, to the cave where Moses had found sanctuary. There came the sound of a still small voice. When Elijah heard it, he went to the mouth of the cave and heard a question. "What are you doing here, Elijah?"

When we are shaken loose of identities and securities that have held us for years, when our lives are overturned, and we find ourselves at the mouth of the cave, the edge of our estate, the boundary between safety and vulnerability, a questioning rises within us, "What are you doing here?" When we teeter on the edge of ecstasy and evil, poised on the epicenter of demonic/angelic powers, the womb of creative/destructive energies, the dark speech of the Spirit whispers to us, "What are you doing here?" God meets us as Elijah, in the sanctuary of our escape agendas, nourishes our vital needs with angel touches, and gives us an engagement agenda, saying "Go and anoint Hazael to be king . . . and Elisha to be prophet. . . ." Go and anoint, lay hands upon, bless, baptize, empower, heal the people and the political/religious systems of your scene. At the heart of a question, a command: go and touch.

Go and touch. Get in touch with your spouse, colleague, father, daughter-in-law, mayor, church, political party, friend. Heal a friendship, anoint an office, bless a bedroom, baptize a work place. One autumn my then ten-year-old son Bob had made the all-star team in his school football. As I rubbed his back while putting him to bed one night, out of the quiet came a still small voice, "Dad, is this the first time you ever rubbed an all-star's back?" I swallowed the lump rising in my throat and said, "Yes, Bob, first time . . . ever." Everyone needs to feel, sometime, somewhere, with someone that one is an all-star, not for doing anything but just for being the person one is. We need to know in our bones that we are all-stars in the hands of our father/mother God. We need the physical reassurance of being touched.

A friend who has lived alone for a long time said, "I suffer from skin hunger." The hunger to be held, cradled, hugged, caressed, touched is human . . . and divine. God also longed to touch us, and so the Word became flesh and dwelt among us. We remember the woman who reached out to touch the hem of Jesus' garment, and the healing energies that flowed between them. We remember the people Jesus touched into new sight, dancing feet, wholeness of every kind. We remember angelic touches we have given and received. We remember the brief embrace of Sadat and Begin—knowing its awkward, ambivalent, ambiguous character—and yearn for broken nations to touch one another into peace. "A touch is worth a thousand words; a kiss, ten thousand."

At the heart of a question, a command: go and touch.

God's Creation Healing

I think that what we suffer in this life can never be compared to
the glory, as yet unrevealed, which is waiting for us. The whole
creation is eagerly waiting for God to reveal his sons. It was not
for any fault on the part of creation that it was made unable to
attain its purpose, it was made so by God; but creation still re-
tains the hope of being freed, like us, from its slavery to deca-
dence, to enjoy the same freedom and glory as the children of
God. From the beginning till now the entire creation, as we
know, has been groaning in one great act of giving birth; and
not only the creation, but all of us who possess the first fruits of
the Spirit, we too groan inwardly as we wait for our bodies to be
set free. For we must be content to hope that we shall be
saved . . . it is something we must wait for with patience.
Romans 8:18–25 (JEB)

May is the kindest month: when orange/black Orioles, indigo
Buntings, rose-breasted Grosbeaks stop by our forest and feeders on their northward journey. We look in our bird log (we
don't have a people log) and note that the Grosbeaks are two
weeks ahead of last year's timetable, and the Bunting is on
schedule to the day. We put out the sunflower seeds and watch
our visitors' dipping/swooping choreography. All is well in the
world again. We take comfort in the turning of the seasons and
the burgeoning truth that "the entire creation is . . . groaning in
one great act of giving birth." And we're part of it, for "we too
groan inwardly as we wait for our bodies to be set free."

For biblical people there is no dichotomy between the God of
history and the God of nature. There is one God over all, in all,
and through all. The sound of Bach and of our own sighing is
also heard in the fluted notes of the Wood Thrush and the
pounding surf of Big Sur. Robert Browning named it "the
C-major of this life."

Hans Kung defines the kingdom of God as "God's Creation
Healed." I like that, and I like it even better as "God's Creation

Healing," acknowledging the process of God's creative power even now healing the earth, history, the nations, us. I can't believe it sometimes, but the return of the Orioles and their friends helps.

As a child I learned many Psalms by heart, among them Psalm 121:1-2 "I will lift up mine eyes unto the hills from whence cometh my help; my help cometh from the Lord who made heaven and earth." When I am afraid, I look around for hills, which remind me that God is still there for us and the cosmos, still healing the creation, even my small part of it. And I take comfort.

Humor and humility both derive from the same root — *humus.* Earth. To be in touch with the earth, as our Native American sisters and brothers have long understood, is to have our souls cleansed of human chauvinism. To be earthy is to enjoy the habits and respect the habitats of our creaturely friends. To be grounded is to slip into a banana peel-perspective which allows us to laugh at ourselves and entertain a self-mockery which keeps us humane. The laughless people are the most dangerous. It is time to explore a theology of pleasure (see Psalm 16). Poor Calvin! He missed so much fun, caused so much work, and forgot altogether about play.

We may think of Jesus, "the son of man," as the offspring of the Human. God is the fully and wholly Human, whose Word became flesh in Jesus and is the militant Word of God in history. Wherever we see seeds of humanity sprouting up from the soil of pain, tears and groaning, we know God is there, healing. A friend wrote, "I am convinced that in these days the gathered congregation, while reassuring and strengthening (and I hope disturbing and enlightening as well), is NOT ENOUGH. Persons of kindred aches and yearnings, of levels of venturing beyond the pack, need each other." Some Mormons and others in Utah ventured beyond the pack and discovered God does not want their holy land to become a network of missile tracks and silos. Other folks are discovering that *all land is holy*, and God doesn't want *any* of it to become a doomsday launch or sponge. The sea is God's, too, and the air. Holy space all.

There is an interlocking of people and place, of person and environment. Love Canal is a cancer in the body of the earth. The nuclear submarine originally named "Corpus Christi" smells with the same rot. Drought discloses that only if we conserve water where we live can those down the river have enough.

Seeds are for sowing. Mustard seeds. Sunflower seeds. The blood of the martyrs (witnesses) is the seed of the church. Seed money is for doing justice, walking humbly with God and loving mercy. Healing mercy. God's creation is healing. Sometimes I can't believe it. But the return of the Orioles and their friends helps. We smile and keep putting out the seeds.

Ambivalent

On the day I called, thou didst answer me.
Thou didst increase my strength of soul.

Psalm 138:3 (RSV)

One winter day on Long Island, while waiting for my wife to conclude a workshop, I drove the twenty minutes to Jones Beach. It was windy and cold. Any place to find shelter on the beach? All the entrances were closed off until I drove by a sign that read "Senior Citizens' Lounge." There was an open road by the sign leading towards the beach. I thought, "I'm fifty-five, almost fifty-six . . . why not?" and drove in. I pushed open the swinging door of the lounge, and looked around the long, narrow room. Couch, chairs, magazines, tables. . . . An old gentleman sat reading a paper. We nodded to each other. I feared he would want to talk but he didn't. Maybe he feared I wanted to talk, but I didn't. I got out my reading materials and journal, and placed my chair near the door where I could look out at the beach and ocean. The sun warmed my face. I leaned back.

Six months since my father's death. Slowly I leafed through my journal notes for those six months. The rolling flow of changes in my family, at Kirkridge, in the nation and world. Job transitions, friendships ended and begun, vocations emerging, nuclear fears rising. And what of my life: stagnation or generativity? Maybe a bit of both. Ambivalence was my word at that retreat last week. Again today in this Senior Citizens' Lounge, I am feeling ambivalent: a middle place of gladness and sadness. Treading water, neither swimming nor sinking. I feel opaque to my inner self, as though there are bunches of insulation around my soul. Everything is muffled, hidden, under wraps, stifled.

Russell Lockhart says that Psyche speaks, Psyche wants to speak. The Spirit moving within me wants to speak. My soul wants to be heard. Mozart is reported as saying that some of his symphonies presented themselves to him; wrote themselves. Is there a song in me presenting itself, a poem that wants to write itself? Speak, Soul, for thy servant wants to hear. Teach me to listen. The psalmist prayed, "On the day I called, Thou didst answer me." The very day. I prayed, "O Lord, increase my strength of soul, today."

Only dreams and poems can help us escape from the power of money, the dread of death, the fear of lies. But my dreams are hidden from me now and my poetry is dried up. "Thou desirest truth in the inward being" (Ps. 51:6). What is the truth of my inward being? Robert Bly writes, "On the borders is where one finds truth; at either side of the border, in this world or the next, there may be certainties or doctrines but not truths."[1] Bereft of certainties, I search for the borders where truth is moving. But I can't get going. My entreprenurial engines are spinning the wheels where there is no soil, no earth-traction, just whining and whirring as on dry cement. Let me stop the spinning, let the engines cool awhile, let me wait. "They that wait upon the Lord shall renew their strength;" their strength of soul. I need strength of soul. (Will vacation yield vocation?)

My mind keeps spinning on the hard surface of things. I feel a journalistic surfeit, a commercial hangover. Emily Dickinson, in her room-tomb, her room-womb, wrote: "The only News I know/is Bulletins all day/From immortality."[2] Some news. I'm not getting news, just information. Facts, not truth. But there is news in Dickinson's poetic bulletins. I've been reading Richard Sewall's rich and learned two-volume book, *The Life of Emily Dickinson*, in recent months. A few pages at night before sleep. I tell my wife I am going to bed with Emily Dickinson. She doesn't appear to be threatened. But I am threatened by those bulletins of truth from the borders of a located life. Psyche speaks to me through her poetry if not my own. Maybe that's enough for now, until the soil of my spirit loosens, once again there is traction for truth, and I shall see visions, and dream dreams as the prophet promised to young and old. O Lord, increase my strength of soul, today.

Hunger for Healing

And a great crowd followed him and thronged about him. And there was a woman who had had a flow of blood for twelve years, and who had suffered much under many physicians, and had spent all that she had, and was no better but rather grew worse. She had heard reports about Jesus, and came up behind him in the crowd and touched his garment. For she said, "If I touch even his garments I shall be made well." And immediately the hemorrhage ceased; and she felt in her body that she was healed of her disease.

Mark 5:24–29 (RSV)

A nameless woman in a crowd. A nobody. Bleeding for twelve years. Doctors, counselors, friends, priests — nobody could help her. The systems of healing had failed her. And not only her. We are also nameless ones. Some of us have been bleeding a long time, and the systems of healing have failed us too. A lot of blood has flowed under the bridges of our lives. Where are you bleeding?

Sometimes I bleed early in the morning when feelings of inadequacy arise within me; I feel that I am "over the hill," or forgotten; or wonder what I am doing out on this mountainside. Our wounds seek a deeper healing than medicines, counseling or therapy can yield. There's a dis-ease in us that hungers for wholeness. Physicians can get at our bodies, psychologists at our psyches, sociologists at our organizational structures, clergy at our faith systems, but who will heal my soul? "Lord, say the word and my soul shall be healed." Every one has a wound that will never fully heal. Where are you bleeding?

That woman came up behind Jesus in the crowd. Not wanting a scene, not wanting to be seen. Just wanting to touch him. How did she know about the sacrament of touch? Who instructed her to trust the healing power of Jesus? Why did her hope endure through all those years of painful disappointment?

57

She didn't ask permission. She just reached out. It took courage. She must have feared being rejected. Yet she hurt and hoped enough to risk reaching out. She touched his garment, and immediately knew in her body that she was healed.

> And Jesus, perceiving in himself that power had gone forth from him immediately turned about in the crowd, and said "Who touched my garments?" And his disciples said to him, "You see the crowd pressing around you, and yet you say, 'Who touched me?'" And he looked around to see who had done it.
>
> *Mark 5:30–32*

"Who touched me?" A nameless woman in a crowd, a nobody—and yet Jesus turned around to see who had touched him. Intimacy in a crowd. There is a difference between *contact*, when people push against one another in a subway, and *touch*. Contact happens in social space, often to our embarrassment or distaste. "Excuse me," we say, to avoid any suspicion or hope that our touching may have been intentional, perhaps even sexual. But Jesus knew there had been a touching. Someone put the touch on him. He was touched.

The Spirit connects us to strangers in a crowd, when eyes meet or gestures are acknowledged. Contact may yield touch. Energy is exchanged and a small healing occurs as the space between two people is humanly warmed. Jesus looked around to see who had touched him, who had claimed his power. He wanted to confirm and complete a mutual acknowledgement of healing power shared. He felt compassion for crowds that are like sheep without a shepherd, and for nameless ones like us who are bleeding internally . . . so far inside, nobody may be able to notice. The incognito Christ is moving in every crowd, waiting to touch and be touched.

The disciples pooh-poohed the episode. Any why not? With all those people pressing, pushing, crowding Jesus, how silly to ask "Who touched me?" "Dozens of people have touched you, Jesus!" People were all over him trying to get close, see, hear. Understandably, Jesus' friends were trying to protect him. These were the same disciples who believed that Jesus had no time for children, and were sure there was no way to feed the five thousand. They were your basic organization people; "can do" folk who know when there's something you can't do.

I identify with them. I have my own agenda well in mind, and I don't want it interrupted, especially by some nobody who has the gall to step into the middle of things and stop the whole show. I've got my eye on the big picture, and don't want to slow down for some small bit of action in one corner. I'm often untouchable, especially by untouchables.

The Church is often an untouchable institution, a place where there's little time for folk who embarrass us with their wounds, their complaints about the healing system having bled them dry, yet left them bleeding. There are congregations where you'd better not talk about some people being divorced, alcoholic, gay or lesbian, feminist, unemployed, because these people are regarded as untouchables, and surely Christ wouldn't have any time for them. Unemployed people often don't go to church because they're ashamed, and don't want to embarrass or upset their friends by their unemployed presence. There are congregations where any talk of nuclear disarmament or comment that the American government is just as likely to make a first missile strike as the Russian government is distinctly in bad taste. Some subjects and situations are untouchable in some churches. What's untouchable in yours?

But the Church is called to be a zone of touching where we are invited to get in touch with one another, God and ourselves. Church is the place where Christ is always looking around to see who is touching him and where the healing power is moving.

> But the woman, knowing what had been done to her, came in fear and trembling and fell down before him, and told him the whole truth. And he said to her, "Daughter, your faith has made you well; go in peace, and be healed of your disease."
> *Mark 5:33–34*

What courage! What grace! She could have just slipped

quietly away. But she knew a miracle of mercy had happened. She knew that a physical and spiritual connection had been made with Jesus. So she came forward. She gave up her privacy. She acknowledged the connection. She went public. And she was scared. She risked ridicule, condemnation, maybe worse. She made public her own healing and the failure of the healing systems.

We too suffer under our healing systems, our national establishment. We spend all we have and are not healed. We reach out to touch the system, only to find that it does not have the power to heal, or that it is in fact untouchable to the likes of us. Only the rich and powerful can put the touch on our system, and they do. But a nation exists to heal the wounds of all of its people, and to prevent them from being further wounded. "For the wound of the daughter of my people is my heart wounded. . . . Is there no balm in Gilead? Is there no physician there?" (Jer. 8:21–22).

There is in fact a bomb in America, and "doctors" here prepare to save us by destroying us. Jesus said, "I came that they may have life" (John 10:10), and gave his life as testimony to his truth. General Electric says, "We bring good things to life," while making profitable purveyors of death, missiles giving the lie to their testimony. Profits eliminate prophets.

Oceans of blood have flowed under the bridges of nationalism. Will our hunger for healing make us go public, bring our dis-ease to the attention of our government? If so, we will not find ourselves alone. More and more people are protesting the brutality of our system on the nameless, powerless poor, and the ultimate human abuse of nuclear war-making. Even in countries where there is no right of petition and assembly, people are going public. Salvadorean peasants, Polish workers, Russian dissidents are being wounded, jailed, imprisoned, tasting death —while making visible the wounding brutality of their systems.

Jesus called her "Daughter." You, too, are a daughter of Abraham and Sarah. You belong. You and I are relatives. We are family. "Whoever does the will of God is my brother and sister and mother" (Mark 3:35). In the family of God, strangers become agents of healing and nameless ones are named daughter, son, sister, brother. Hearts hallowed by truth-telling are healed. We know we are accepted by One whose grace flows through our fear and trembling.

"Go in peace" is the word of commissioning. It is the word to leave, to grow up, and to go out.

O Lord, say the word and our souls and bodies and systems shall be healed. Touch us and we shall be made well. Grant us Your peace that we may go forth in gladness, fearing not to uncover the bloody systems which wound us and our sisters and brothers. Thank you for the faith of that nameless woman, Your daughter, our sister. Give us such faith.

Amen.

The Face of my Secret Heart

Behold, thou desirest truth in the inward being;
therefore teach me wisdom in my secret heart.
Psalm 51:6 (RSV)

I sought the Lord, and he answered me,
and delivered me from all my fears.
Look to him, and be radiant;
so your face shall never be ashamed.
Psalm 34:4–5 (RSV)

It is late afternoon. It is mauve in the valley below. Friends have gathered in our living room. The time of wine and cheese and conversation is ending. People are settling now in chairs or on pillows in front of the coal stove. We have invited them to share a period of common quiet, while listening to music. This corporate quiet is a Kirkridge tradition, begun by the Platts, a Quaker couple who built and lived in their own house at Kirkridge, naming it *Quiet Ways*. The common quiet allows a gathering and centering community, a deepening together, a spiraling down into the truth of our inward being. I love these times.

The bustle is subsiding. People are letting themselves let down, let go, let be. It is good to be relieved of talking and listening to talking. There is a blessedness about the silence. I put the turntable on, and play the Schubert *Impromptus.* I lean back and listen to the tendering, gentling sound. I close my eyes and sink into the silence. After a time, I open my eyes and look around the room.

Amazing faces. Now in repose. The sound of the music, the warmth of the wine, the safety of the silence — have released our inner yearnings. There is an unacknowledged but intuitive intimacy. The face guards have gently fallen away, and there are the faces of the secret heart. Grave faces. Now vulnerable. Faces desperate, sad, weary, betrayed, ashamed—weathered into those wrinkles which are "the credentials of humanity."

Amazing confessions written from chin to hairline. Burdens being laid down, pain yielded from its private prison. Radiant sorrow. Suffering dignity. The sounding music washes away the cosmetic guises to reveal the face of the secret heart, the truth of the inward being. I bow my head lest I intrude on precious revelations unintended or unknown. I will not prey upon such faces, but pray for their owners. I wonder if any one has seen the face of my secret heart? And what such a one has seen there. Perhaps someone has a truth-gift for me.

These faces shine with a terrible beauty. They invite respect and compassion. We belong to one another. Though we will not acknowledge it easily, there is an ease in this quiet communion. I want it to go on. I savor it. I am grateful to be where I am, with these friends, and who I am in this house. We are sharing a healing, a peacemaking of the soul. I pray:

> Lord, thank You for the inner wisdom You are allowing us to make visible together. Thank You for these dear, searching, hurting, and yearning friends. Thank You for the flowing sound, the lonely tears, the glad silence. Comfort us all. Caress our souls with Your kindly Spirit. Breathe through our bruised bodies fresh life and health. Heal our hearts. Forgive our faces.

The music ends. Smiles are shared. The bustle begins. We move away from the miracle of the commonwealth in the common quiet.

It is early evening.

Coming Out

Now when Jesus came, he found that Lazarus had already been in the tomb four days. . . . Then, Mary, when she came where Jesus was and saw him, fell at his feet, saying to him, "Lord, if you had been here, my brother would not have died." When Jesus saw her weeping, and the Jews who came with her also weeping, he was deeply moved in spirit and troubled; and he said, "Where have you laid him?" They said to him, "Lord, come and see." Jesus wept. . . . Then Jesus, deeply moved again, came to the tomb; it was a cave, and a stone lay upon it. Jesus said, "Take away the stone." Martha, the sister of the dead man, said to him, "Lord, by this time there will be an odor, for he has been dead four days." . . . they took away the stone . . . Jesus . . . cried out with a loud voice, "Lazarus, come out." The dead man came out, his hands and feet bound with bandages, and his face wrapped with a cloth. Jesus said to them, "Unbind him, and let him go."

John 11:14–44 (RSV)

There was grieving to do. Someone was dead. When Jesus saw Mary and her friends weeping, he was deeply moved. He went to the tomb and burst into tears.

There was grieving to do, not only for Lazarus, but for Jesus. He was on his own journey to the death, on the way to Gethsemane. There is grieving to do for ourselves. Something is ending for us too.

Jesus said to them, "Take away the stone." Martha objected on grounds that the body had been in the tomb four days and that there would be an odor. A four-day stench.

What would it be like to be Lazarus, lying in that cave? In what way have we died or are we dying? Who is weeping for us? What does our cave feel and look like? Is it earthy and damp, or is it like dry bones and stale air? Are we afraid in there, or sad, or bitter? What is our four-year or forty-year stench?

Consider an existential theory, after Descartes: *being as on-*

ion. "I stink, therefore I am." I am a stinker. (Better to be a stinker than not to be at all!) Something is rotten in the state of my life. Something is rotting in my roles and relationships. Something is decaying in my soul. There is a stink in the systems and institutions that imprison me. And Martha is right. It could be embarrassing to go public, to bring it out into the open.

Sometimes my faith stinks of ideology. When a certain button gets pushed in me, passion overwhelms reason, and I get angry at those who disagree with me. I regress to a good guys/bad guys (lack of) perspective. My particular vision turns out to be partial, as always. And again I must struggle towards a passionate detachment, not without embarrassment.

What is your special stink? What is embarrassing about your style of living? What would be embarrassing about you if it came out? Would *you* be embarrassing if you came out? And what is the stone that keeps you inside, the external barrier you can't remove or think you can't remove?

There is grieving to do.

There is also birthing to do. Someone is being raised from the dead. Grieving and birthing. "They took away the stone." It is the role of friends, family, and church to help remove the external barriers that prevent our liberation and healing. Who might help remove the stone for you? Whose stone might you help to roll away?

Then Jesus "cried out with a loud voice." Jesus didn't whisper or quietly beckon. He shouted. It must have shocked people. Couldn't he keep this thing quiet, private? Yet, birth is painful and public. Birthing means bleeding, sweating, crying out. We don't come gently into this good day, but raging, wrenching at the light! No way to keep a birthing hidden or decorous. Resurrection is an earthshaking matter. "And behold, the curtain of the temple was torn in two, from top to bottom; and the earth shook, and the rocks were split" (Matt. 27:51). Resurrection is a political event, grounds for going to jail. "The priests and the captain of the temple and the Sadducees came upon them, annoyed because they were . . . proclaiming in Jesus the resurrection from the dead. And they arrested them and put them in custody . . ." (Acts 4:1-3).

Jesus cried out with a loud voice, "Lazarus, come out!" This is a blessed name-calling. A biblical name-calling. "Fear not, for I have redeemed you; I have called you by name, you are mine" (Is. 43:1). "Lazarus," "Bob," "Anne, come out!" Come out, no matter what we have done or not done, no matter how much of a stinker we may be or think we are. The Good Shepherd knows our name and calls us by name.

A child living in New Haven, Connecticut, once prayed the Lord's Prayer to her mother in this fashion: "Our Father who art in New Haven, how did you know my name?" A child's wisdom. Christ comes to us where we are living and dying. Christ calls our name. Christ calls us in our stench. Will the real John Jones please stand up! Will the real Mary Brown please stand up! Come out. Come out of hiding. Come out of the closet.

There are many closets and many ways of coming out. A gay or lesbian person comes out of the closet of a false heterosexuality. A divorcing person comes out of the closet of a dying marriage. A peacemaker comes out of the closet of a rotting militarist mindset. A whistleblower comes out of the closet of a corrupt institution or system.

Coming out has to do with undertaking one's true vocation, regardless of what "they" think. Coming out makes a disturbance and lets out a stink. Coming out is going public. It is being on the outside what one is on the inside. Maybe it's time for us to stand up and be counted and accountable.

Wallace Stevens wrote:

> Throw away the lights, the definitions
> and say of what you see in the dark
> That it is this or that
> But do not use rotted names
> Nothing must stand
> Between you and the shapes you take
> When the crust of shape has been destroyed.[1]

No longer will we use rotted names, but real names, our real names. Integrity is better than success; honesty of more value than respectability. "Lazarus, come out!"

The bad news is that we *won't* come out; the good news is that most of us *can* come out. We can obey the call. We can undertake our vocation. We can choose to leave the tomb we're in. Most of us can say Yes with our feet, take the first step out.

Jesus said, "Unbind him and let him go." There is the ministry of unbinding one another, of letting people go. There is a Moses ministry here, not only for individuals, but for families, institutions, churches, systems, nations. "Let my people go." Dismantel the chains of oppression. Disassemble the economic and political arrangements that make and keep people poor and on the outside, in order to make a healthy reassembling. The church is called to take the bandages from bondage, to unwrap the stinking constraints, so that we may become healed and healers in the fresh air of freedom. Sometimes the church must unwrap its own tangled tradition in order to uncover its truth. What systems will you help to unbind?

The dead man came out. That's good news! If a dead man can come out, you and I can come out. We too can say "Yes" to the gospel imperative. Even if we come out wrapped in grave clothes, under wraps. We have been wrapped, weighted down with vestments and investments laid upon us by others and accepted by ourselves. Will our friends help us take off these wraps, or in fact, can we throw them off ourselves? We are going to a party, a "come-out-as-you-are" party, a "just-as-I-am" party. It's like a debut, when a new adult is about to meet the world. Are we ready to make our debut, alive again, stumbling awake into our new freedom? There is birthing to do. Someone is alive.

How Awesome
Is This Place!

Jacob left Beersheba, and went toward Haran. And he came to a certain place, and stayed there that night, because the sun had set. Taking one of the stones of that place, he put it under his head and lay down in that place to sleep. And he dreamed that there was a ladder set up on the earth, and the top of it reached to heaven.... Then Jacob awoke from his sleep and said, "Surely the Lord is in this place; and I did not know it." And he was afraid and said, "How awesome is this place! This is none other than the house of God, and this is the gate of heaven." So Jacob rose early in the morning, and he took the stone which he had put under his head and set it up for a pillar and poured oil on the top of it. He called the name of that place Bethel....

Genesis 28:10–22 (RSV)

Throughout human history, people have set up stones to identify those special places where holy revelations have happened. Stones with stories to tell. There are the stones of Stonehenge and Chartres: known to the world, honored for their mystery and beauty, hallowed for the presence of God in their silent dignity down the centuries. There are the stones of other more humble monuments or buildings: unknown but to a few who treasure the presence of God become real in that place.

The hearthstones of the Kirkridge Farmhouse were set up in 1815. For more that 125 years, farm families cooked their food, read their books, and warmed their bodies at that hearth. In the last forty years, countless people have made pilgrimages to sit before those stones, listening for their silent stories; telling their own.

It is a strange grace whereby a particular group of individuals decide to make this pilgrimage, at this time, with these people. Beneath our several, conscious agendas, the Spirit is moving: disrupting, integrating, sighing, breathing. The outward journey triggers the possibility of an inner one. The soil of our lives is jostled by the journeying, and we are freshly permeable to the sifting, seeding Spirit. What stories are frozen in these stones: stories of confessions heard, wounds healed, songs shared, friendships sealed? What stories are frozen in these stoney hearts, stories which may yet emerge from warmed hearts? Is this a house of God? Is the Lord truly in this place?

What are the houses, buildings, stones which mark holy space for you? Where has God become manifest to you in such manner that you were amazed by grace, knew the Presence, and wanted to mark the memory? Is there a house, a church building, a workspace, a bedroom, a kitchen, a street, a mountain, a city, a desert, a beach where you have been visited by a strange Spirit? René Dubos wrote that when the words *genius* or *spirit* are used to denote the distinctive characteristics of a given region, city, institution or place, there is implied "the tacit acknowledgment that each place possess a set of attributes that determines the uniqueness of its landscape and its people."[1] San Francisco and Boston, for example, despite the changes in each city over the centuries, retain their own unique genius, spirit, flavor — that enduring ambiance of tangible character that is both given and made. Dubos is speaking of the significance of place. Places where pillows become pillars, bushes begin burning, and earth is filled with treasure. Stones with stories to tell.

The Kirkridge Farmhouse is built on a hillside of the Appalachian ridge; these ancient stones thrust up here some thirty million years ago. Once the Lenape Indians roamed, hunted and fished here. That Native American dignity abides on the mountainside, though wounded by more recent excavations, building, and tree cutting. Still, these are hills "whence cometh our help" and the help is still coming. The stones glow with stories. These dining room tables become Emmaus tables where our hearts and eyes are opened and we know the Lord has surely been among us. How awesome is this place! Carved into the wooden mantlepiece of another Pennsylvania farmhouse built in 1750 and now become an Inn, are words of the poet Horace:

Ille Terrarum Mihi Prater Omnes Angulus Ridet. (This corner of the earth smiles on me above all others.)

In the silent dark around the hearth, there are those who rejoice in this corner of the earth. I marvel at these old rafter beams, and all they have heard and seen, welcomed and witnessed. A cloud of witnesses indeed. The spirits of those gone before us now abiding in the mystery of beam and stone, our spirits touching theirs. A comfort to know we do not make our journey alone, but are surrounded and supported by all the saints. A cloud of witnesses above and below. Joyce Timpanelli writes, "The dead are holding hands under the earth."[2] Under the earth. We are standing on their shoulders. We depend on them and they support us. It is the custom of the Moravians in Bethlehem, Pennsylvania to gather on Easter morning in the great graveyard by the Mother Church, and sing praises to the risen Christ whose people are being raised from the dead.

The modesty of this place. It is comfortable here. One can let the roles and masks slip off here in the dark, without being noticed for awhile. It seems a safe and blessed place. "In every place where I cause my name to be remembered I will come to you and bless you." Lord, come to us and bless us. There are angels here, but demons too. This is a place to let demons out and wrestle them to a painful blessing, a place in which to acknowledge wounds and share them. In the sharing is the healing. Pilgrim souls are restored as strangers find welcome. This is a place of ease and gentle care. A place for taking care. A place for turning corners or discovering you have turned one. A place where the blurred slide of your life can slip or pop into focus. A place in which to laugh, weep, sing, maybe even dance, and surely, pray. Surely, the Lord is in this place. How awesome is this place!

Notes

SINKING INTO GOD
1. Matthew Fox, *Breakthrough: Meister Eckhart's Creation Spirituality in New Translation* (Garden City, New York: Doubleday, 1977), pp. 179-180.
2. Jacob Boehme, *The Way to Christ* in *The Classics of Western Spirituality* (New York: Paulist Press, 1978), p. 43.

THE RESTORATION OF ALL THINGS
1. Dietrich Bonhoeffer, *Letters and Papers from Prison* (New York: Macmillan, 1953).
2. *New York Times* news article.
3. John Cole, *New York Times* article, op-ed page.
4. H. Richard Niebuhr, *The Responsible Self* (New York: Harper & Row, 1963), p. 177.

SIGNS
1. Sir Bernard Lovell, *New York Times Magazine* article.
2. Ibid.

THE WORD IS VERY NEAR TO YOU
1. Albert Camus quoted by Norman Cousins in an editorial entitled "Confrontation" in *Saturday Review*, March 25, 1961, p. 32.
2. Abraham Joshua Heschel, *Man's Quest for God* (New York: Charles Scribner's Sons, 1954), p. 12.
3. Ibid., p. 11.

YESTERDAY'S WILL OF GOD
1. *New York Times* article, March 31, 1975, p. 38.

HO—PING
1. Richard Barnet, *The Lean Years* (New York: Simon and Schuster, 1980).

DO YOU WANT TO BE HEALED?
1. Morton Kelsey in a presentation at a Kirkridge retreat.
2. Ibid.

THE ART OF LEAVING
1. Henri Nouwen, *The Living Reminder* (New York: Seabury Press, 1977), p. 44.
2. Ibid., p. 39.
3. Alan Paton, "Meditation for a Young Boy Confirmed" in *The Christian Century*, 1954.

GO UP INTO THE GAPS
1. Annie Dillard, *Pilgrim At Tinker Creek* (New York: Harper Magazine Press, 1974).
2. Dietrich Bonhoeffer, *Letters and Papers from Prison* (New York: Macmillan, 1953).

INVESTING IN GOD'S FUTURE
1. William Stringfellow in a presentation at a Kirkridge retreat.

DRAGONS AND PRINCESSES
1. Rainer Maria Rilke, *Letters to a Young Poet*, trans. M.D. Herter Norton (New York: W.W. Norton, 1934).

AMBIVALENT
1. Robert Bly, *Truth Barriers*, trans. Robert Bly (New York: Harper & Row).
2. Emily Dickinson, quoted by Richard B. Sewall in *The Life of Emily Dickinson* (New York: Farrar, Straus and Giroux, 1974).

COMING OUT
1. Wallace Stevens, *The Collected Poems of Wallace Stevens* (New York: Alfred A. Knopf, 1976).

HOW AWESOME IS THIS PLACE
1. Rene Dubos, *A God Within* (New York: Charles Scribner's Sons, 1972), pp. 6-7.
2. Joyce Timpanelli, *Stones for the Hours of the Night* (New York: Rapoport Printing Corporation, 1978).

PRAYERS

I Offer Myself

Lord,
I offer my needs to you
all that affects my health
I offer my wants to you
all the range of my reaching
I offer my oughts to you
all the duties that define my life
I offer my loves to you
all the people for whom I care

Help me to understand what I need
for my own survival
and what I can get along without
Help me to find a healthy balance
between my wants and my oughts
and give me the wisdom to know
you are in both
Heal and hallow all my loves
that my caring may be
clear and honest

Help me discern when I should
deny myself
for the sake of others
and when I must
affirm myself
for my own sake

I long for leading
I wish the decision
would make itself
I can't meet everybody's
expectations
I can't prevent everyone's hurts

What matters most?
No one can tell me
No one

I have to decide alone

Lord,
I offer myself to you

Stretch Our Sympathies

Lord, we yearn towards people
  whose faces are strange to us
     faces crying over coffins
     faces staring out of barred windows
   child faces innocent in danger
     aged faces pleated with patience

Deliver us from pride of achievement
to reach out
to those whose need
beckons

Deliver us from self-preoccupation
to occupy ourselves
with neighbors
far
and
near

Kindle our kindness
Bend our reluctance

Draw us beyond the small circle of
"my kind"
to the large circle of
mankind

Stretch our sympathies
and our dollars
to the measure of
human need

Have I Crossed My Rubicon?

Have I crossed my Rubicon?
a border is frightening
back is home
beyond is homeless
security is behind
uncertainty is ahead
     look forward,
          then
          now

Have I crossed my Rubicon?
I'm afraid
to risk everything
for the unknown
courage
costs more than
caution
but promises more

Have I crossed my Rubicon?
new life
is threat
as well as
promise
end
as well as
beginning

Have I crossed my Rubicon?
faith
is stronger than
fear
my time is coming
the time to cross
not without
fear

> look forward,
>> then
>> now

Interrogation

> Something there is in me
>> that makes for a mob
> something cowardly
>> that gangs up on a man
>> when he's down
>> especially an enemy,
>>> or competitor
>>> or outsider

> Something there is in me
>> that puts a finger to the wind
> something cold
>> that washes my hands of a loser
>> and gives the people
>> what they want

> Something there is in me
>> that defends
>> the defenseless
> something tough
>> that comes out tender
>> to comfort the casualty
>> or protect the protester

> it's cruel
> but common
>> to play cat and mouse
>> with people
> it's cruel
> but common

to be on the carpet
and have the rug pulled out
to be at bay
> before a boss
>> or a board

a prisoner
discovers his own mettle
in the moment of
interrogation
> when truth
> is sought
> or bought
>> by terror

Am I a prisoner?
Who interrogates me?
Whom do I interrogate?

The truth
that a man is
becomes visible
when Power
has him by the
throat

Stretch Our Energies

Lord, we yearn for our country

> so rich in good will
> so torn with greed and fear

> so blessed with resources
> so in love with power

> so innocent
> so corrupt

Give us eyes and spirit to discern

truth from propaganda
integrity from image
compassion from rhetoric
wisdom from information

Help us to

take responsibility for our power
admit our mistakes
forgive one another

and
Stretch our energies

towards our own healing
and the healing of humanity

When the Sunlight Comes

The ice stretched across the river
almost to the west bank
where a few yards of water were flowing free.
It made me think of my own life:
much of it frozen over, covered, stable, dependable,
yet movement and flux nearby.
How the currents swirl under the ice.
A little sunlight can melt it all in a few hours,
to flow free, fast, and newly alive.

I think of my friend at lunch,
listening to his story,
discovering how much is going on under the ice.
I felt kinship with him,
struggling, stretching.
How will it be with him when the sunlight comes,
the ice breaks up,
and things flow free, fast, and newly alive?

Just when I think I have it all together
it begins to come apart somewhere;
and just when everything seems to be falling to pieces
there is a quiet place and a knitting.
I want so much not to miss the beauty, the love,
the meaning of it all.
I yearn for a kind of communication
with those I love
that is unarmored,
without special motive,
clear and caring.
How will it be with me when the sunlight comes,
the ice breaks up
and things flow free, fast, and newly alive?

Faces of the Forgotten

God,
Your heart
must break
when you see
the faces of the forgotten
  hidden in the hills
  huddled in hotels
  and nursing homes
tucked in tenements
stranded in the station
  or on the street

Bless all the lonely people
comfort them with kind
  relatives, friends, doctors, social workers, policemen

move us
 to be willing
 to reorder our priorities
 to tax ourselves enough
 to seek and find
  the welfare of the city
  where you have sent us

You know
what it's like
to be
rejected
neglected
homeless
hopeless
deserted

That comforts me
Let me comfort
 all the lonely people
I know

The Secret Places

I CALL TO YOU
FROM THE secret PLACES
OF MY SOUL

 HEAR MY ACHE
 TOUCH MY FEAR
 SEE MY SORROW
 TASTE MY REMORSE

YOU CALL TO ME
FROM THE secret PLACES
OF MY SOUL

 HEAR MY HEALING
 TOUCH MY COMFORT

SEE MY WISDOM
TASTE MY PARDON

DEEP CALLS TO DEEP
IN THE secret PLACES
OF MY SOUL

Shelter

water running down the airplane window
like tears
people walking with umbrellas
for shelter

shelter
I need
shelter
Lord

heal the wounds
of those I have wounded
and my wounds

lead me
walk beside me
follow me

let forgiveness
take my arms
and hope
invite my feet

shelter us all
toward a
time
of
safety
and
confidence

Too Busy To Listen?

I feel for parents
   who want to enjoy their children
   but don't know how
   who do their best
   but fail
   and don't know
   why
   it happened

I feel for kids
   who are no longer
   kids
   who want to enjoy their parents
   but can't
   who would rather stay home
   but have to leave
   or would rather leave home
   but have to stay
     in order to keep alive

Why is it so hard to listen?

Sometimes
when I try to listen
to my kids
I lose patience
   jump to conclusions
   criticize their friends
   don't understand
Sometimes
   I could cry
   we get so mad
     so quickly
   about so little

Maybe
　　listening
　　is the most important part of
　　loving

Please!
　　let me listen
　　while there's still time
　　before the kids start
　　　　　　　leaving home

A Strange Joy

Heart
reaching
empty and
hungry
hoping

Mind
wondering
wild and
restless
groping

Body
aching
desire
prisoned-in-flesh
roaring

Soul
stretching
strong
a strange joy
soaring

If I Am Making A Mistake

O God
if I am making a mistake
let me know
before it's too late

I'm afraid

sometimes
I wish that circumstances
or other people
or Somebody
would settle things for me
one way or the other

sometimes
I wish you would open or shut
a door
but I know I will still
have to choose
between doors
and
the best parts of me
don't want to give up that freedom

I want happiness for all those I care about
and my own happiness
Is there any way
happiness can happen for all?

is my fear only natural
as I reach the final turning
begin to taste my losses
and know in my insides
that things will never be the same again?

or is my fear a red light from you?

or
both?

Only in you
can I find peace without
threat
only with you
can I dare to choose
and make myself
so vulnerable

I
am
safe
with
you

I Love the Mystery

standing on the deck late at night
looking into the glittering dark
my friend said
    "I love the mystery
    I don't have to know
    who or what it is"

yes
I too love the mystery
and profess to know
who and what it is
    "the God of Abraham, Isaac and
Jacob
    the Father of our Lord Jesus Christ"

yet
I am uneasy
with quick, definite name tags
for the Nameless One

there is Christian closure
with God

which sometimes is
too certain
    smug
    familiar
    finished
for me

today
I feel more akin to
Abraham and Jacob
than to
Peter and Paul

more a pilgrim
than a disciple
more a seeker
than a finder
more a learner
than a teacher

    "Lo, I tell you a mystery"

but the mystery is larger
than the telling
it eludes our boundaries
it escapes our
    taming
    and
    naming

I love the mystery

Why Have You Left Me Alone?

I feel like a motherless child
I can't go home again
it's too late
I'm too old
my parents can't understand me
nor my spouse, children, friends

I share a part of myself
with this person
another part with that person
but my whole self
with no one

my individuality
clarifies and sharpens
but is itself
a bar
a fence
a wall

am I unwilling to be known
or afraid
or just don't know how?

Augustine prayed:
"our hearts are restless
'til they find their rest in Thee"

will I always be alone
in this life?

Jesus was lonely
"foxes have holes, birds of the air have nests,
but I have no place to lay my head."

Jesus was alone
"my God, my God, why have you left me alone?"

there is no answer to that question
this side of death
for Jesus
or me
or anyone

Lord
help me live my loneliness
by accepting it

let your comfort come to me
and your assurance steal over me
that my heart may come to rest
in you
for a moment
or a little longer

Don't Play Hooky

my friend said to me:

God is working in the loosening of your life
    emptying you of certainties
  breaking your self-image
      as a man who could never choose this
      or would always do that
  making you suffer the loneliness
    of having escaped your own skin
  crowding you with the presence
    of an inner stranger
for you do not yet know yourself

Don't play hooky from God now
    don't pray just for others
    pray for yourself
that you may be able to trust God
    working in the dark of you
that you may be willing to
    experience the pain of his presence
not evading or avoiding
what matters now is not whether
    you were disobedient
    or obedient
    or confused

what matters now is that
    the old images are breaking
    your images of yourself
        other selves
        the will of God

God is kneading you like clay
molding your stubborn will
to be supple in his spirit
let him shape you

there is coming to you
the grace of a new
self-understanding
perhaps even
the peace of a new
self-acceptance

you will be learning
who you are
all by
yourself

In the Dark

In the dark
that's where I am
it's so easy to
see into someone else's dark
so hard to
see in my own dark

How I love being
with my child

in the silent companionship
of trust
together
I who am wise as a serpent
and do not understand
she who is innocent as a dove
and sees in the dark

Is it that I like the dark
and its hidden mysteries
or
am I bored with the light
and its revealed certainties

Have I lost my way
or chosen my way
Am I lost
or could I
find my way out of the dark
if I wanted to

What is it I don't understand:
my friend-enemy?
myself?
Do I want to understand
myself
or am I hiding in the dark

God, I am comforted
to know that
You know
me Yet You don't condemn me
You could
others do
I do myself, sometimes

I seem able to defend myself
against condemnation
it's understanding that
undermines
my not understanding
till I begin to
understand

Who Am I When I Am Not Working?

A lack of energy loosens me this morning
I am waiting for my life to catch up with me
a fallow time

The injunction to get busy and produce
still pokes me
but I am smiling at it today

Being out of harness
and losing my grip on routine
threatens
but also
intrigues me

Who am I when I am not working?
I don't know
but it's time I found out

The Time of Self-Knowledge

I have a friend by the name of Murtha
who had a plaque on his door
which read
"Murtha Here"

Henri Nouwen wrote:
"to be at home in your own house
means to discover the center of your life
in your own heart"

One day I sat in my study
and let a few words
taste
resonate
penetrate
> *let me live in peace*
> *at home with You*
> *all the days of my life*

I let those words sink down
and dwell in my private space
bringing quietness
and confidence
for a time

Heschel wrote:
"the words of the liturgy
are footholds for the soul"

Sometimes
words of Scripture, hymn, or prayer
are footholds for my soul
becoming flesh in me
leavening my inner space

I need such times of concentration
when the particles of the self
move into alignment
when I can be at home
with myself

Raines here

Here I Am

Here I am
clay
to shape
and
be shaped
to master
and be mastered

turning
whirling
stuff of
past/future
where I come from
where I'm going
alpha
and
omega
world without end Amen

But not yet
now
still stretching
neither beyond
nor below
but rising
yeast of God
yearning escape
in formlessness
learning freedom
in form

Miracle
of
me
in
Your hands
broken

Once More

Lord of little things
   you made your home
   in a stable under a star
   in a cradle on straw
and the little things
shone their starlit welcome
   make your home with me
   in the little things of my days
   cards, gifts, mistletoe on tiptoe
   tree tinsel, multicolored lights
and let the little things
shine their glory for you and me
once more

Lord of little creatures
   you made your home
   in a shelter for animals
   attended by donkey and ox,
   also sheep on a near hillside
and the little creatures
sounded their earthy welcome
   make your home with me
   and the little creatures of my days
   now that the ducks have gone
   and the wild geese,
   waken me to the wildness
   my rabbit-running, deer-leaping heart

comfort me with the affectionate pawing
of my dog, or the purring of my cat
delight me with the bird-flutter
at my feeder, and
the wings swooping low over rooftops
and let the little creatures
sound their earthy angel-song for you and me

Lord of little people
  you made your home
  with peasant parents
  nameless shepherds, gifted searchers
and the little people
reached out to touch you
  in wondering welcome
make your home with me
  and the little people of my days
  star-eyed children peeking, hiding
  grown-up children loving, lonely
  white-haired children, remembering, yearning
sit with me in the empty chair at the table
meet me in the postman at the door
stand beside me in the friendship of the years
and let the little people reach their arms
  around you and me
once more

Lord of little me
  you made your home
  in the heart of my world
  make your home now
  in the world of my heart
Love me lonely
only loving you.

Welcome little Lord
Lord of little me
Once more.

I Long To Be Known By My Children

Sun pouring in the large east windows
I started the coffee
shook seed into the bird feeders
and walked down below the house
into the long cut to the salt block
clear hoofmarks in the mud
deer

I stood alone
satisfied
air cold and quiet on my face

sadness crept in

I looked at my children's picture this morning
I miss them so
the dailiness of living in the same house
the time when we were a happy family together

I long to be known by my children
not just as their father
but as I am in my own self
with my strengths and weaknesses
without pretense or apology
known in my humanness

I find myself relating to them now
no longer as a family group
but one to one
to each as an individual
exchanging letters with each
discovering the ways in which
each relationship is unique
to be understood, shared, and fostered
in particular ways
not fearing the diversity
but enjoying it

the parental role abides
the personal knowing deepens
I long to be known by my children

I stand alone by the salt block
and think of each child
pray for each one
and for myself
not without tears
and smiles

Limits

people like me
want and need limits
within which to feel secure
against which to find
our own identity
distance
privacy

people like me
strain to set up our lives
and those of others
with prescriptions
so that we can manage
if not control them

people like me
have to exceed limits
to define our inner direction
to become strong enough
in our own eyes
to use limits
as clues
and no longer
as bonds

we need to develop "do's"
so compelling
we can survive the "don'ts"

people like me
make agendas
for ourselves and others
uneasy with ambiguity
we seek certainty
insecure with open-endedness
we seek early closure
we are afraid
to trust and to believe

> Lord
> make me graceful
> within limits
> and
> without limits
> let me be
> at ease with my own direction
> sensitive to that of others
> respectful of customs and procedures
> patient towards my own unfolding
> trusting where I cannot manage
> believing where I cannot see

Bittersweet Is Beautiful

Bittersweet is beautiful
in its time
            is love lost
or remembered
            is wanting
this time
for all time
      as time goes by
with time on my hands

Are my times in Your hand,
O Lord?

Beautiful is bittersweet
in its time
               is wanting to
kill time
        so as to save time
           and to have time
        to hold my beloved
        against the time
           as time marches on
        with my beloved in my arms
Is my beloved in Your arms,
O Lord?

        O bitter is the beauty
           when tender is the time!

My Frail Raft

I love walking at the river alone
it is quiet there
the river flowing on
ever on
like my life

               You are with me
               beside still waters
               near swift waters
               in the rapids
               in the quiet

Grant me in my frail raft
not to struggle
against the current of your leading
but to yield
to the flow of your pressure

You are with me
beside still waters
near swift waters
in the rapids
in the quiet

Let pressure from within
yield clarity
let pressure from without
distill patience
let me sense in every pressure
your presence

You are with me
beside still waters
near swift waters
in the rapids
in the quiet

I Am Happening

There is in me a process of
renascence

the shadow side emerging
my demons surfacing
to join my angels
discovering my dark power of being
unlocking the inner self

there is a strange momentum
about what is happening
in me

I am in gestation
giving birth to myself
yielding self-knowledge

it is a time for quiet eyes
a time to be simple
                private
                    rooted
a time to follow the meaning
and trust it

I believe
God is in what is happening
in me

I am being freed from the past
with appreciation
and freed for the future
with readiness

a particular hope is shaping
a careful joy is rising

don't hurry it
don't analyze it

it is being given
even as
it is being received

I am happening

Let Our Vision Reach

O Lord
refresh our hopes for ourselves
and our nation.
We are troubled and bewildered.
We see corruption in high places
and know that we ourselves are not immune
to the temptations of power
or the corrosions of privilege.
We see narrow interests prevail
over larger loyalties,

and we would have our own loyalties
set in order
and our own priorities
brought to focus.

Give those in authority over us
grace to do those things
which will invite confidence in their office
and trust in themselves.
Let not a spirit of vindictiveness
make us vengeful towards
those who do wrong,
but let us pursue justice with mercy
as those who know that we ourselves
are not without sin.

Let our vision reach beyond the next deal,
the next election,
to that truth which alone can set us free,
and that candor which alone can restore our trust.
If we have become wise as serpents
restore also to us the innocence of doves
that we be neither bitter nor cynical
but aware of our frailty
and the frailty of all people,
modest in the assumption of our virtue
generous in affirming the virtue of others.

Lift us beyond our own immediate advantage
that we may come to the aid of
those who are without power to exercise their liberty
and those who are without liberty to exercise their power.
Renew in us a soaring spirit
and restore to us that vision without which we perish
that walking together in justice
we may make peace on earth.
Amen.

My Arms Are Hungry

Lord
bless my dear children
help me accept the loss of
seeing their faces
hearing their voices
feeling their arms
My arms are hungry for them

Let me not hold back my tears
but let them freely flow
as the release of my sorrow
May your tender mercy
ease the pain of my heart
and heal its wounds

Take my might-have-beens
and place them gently aside
in my life's journey
as way stations
I have left behind
And after grieving
may I look to the new days
in glad hope

Let the meanings gather
let me be deepened
tendered
tempered

Let the judgmental spirit in me
be broken
as I am broken
as the bread is broken
for
me

The Silent Father

Is it You
who wakes me
in the darkness
to cry
without tears

Is it You
who forces me
to learn
through my own pain
of the pain
of others

You are cruel
to teach me
with silence
I am afraid
of silence
I want
answers, reasons
But You are silent
not absent
but silent
Why?
Will you kill me
with silence
my Father?

Yet
You do not leave me
    alone
You come to me
You strengthen me
You provide for me
You do not remove
    my pain or fear
    but

You help me bear it
   and grow tender
You are teaching me
to trust You
   in the silence
and I am learning
                  so slowly
there is kindness
in your cruelty

I hear You
in the sounds of
silence

A Tougher Sense of Self

Am I more concerned with
strategy
than conviction

with what others think
than what I think?

Does my need for approval
cause me to bend myself out of shape
to please others?

Lord
give me a careful reticence
in my expressions of
love for others
that none may feel
unduly bound by obligation
nor tied to expectation
give me a tougher sense of self
that I may value
truth
as much as love

intellect
as much as emotion
honesty
as much as community

I would value
substance
more than appearance
strategy
less than conviction

So Lonely Sometimes

So lonely sometimes
yearning toward each other
so near
so far

We're hurting, Lord
heal us

> Let cheeks be radiant
> again and warm
> Let us hear those belly laughs
> Let the looks and touches of love
> be tender
> Let us be gentle with each other
> and patient with ourselves

Spring us loose from yesterday
to trust tomorrow
knowing that in all we are and do
You are with us to the end
and to the beginning again

Hold
us
close
   and
      set us free
to hold
each other
   and
      to let each other go

Fear of the Unknown

I'm trying to figure out
what scares me

A friend wrote me
that he was angry
at something I did
and he is a peaceful man
and
I was shocked, then scared,
that I could get such a man
angry at me
Things were not
what they had seemed to be
I was not
what I had seemed to me
and to him
to be
My world was called
into question

Do You meet me
in what scares me?

Is it You
who calls me
into question
and scares me
into the possibility
of becoming a blind man
who sees that he can't see

Fear of You
is the beginning
of wisdom, they say...
Is it fear
of the unknown I'm in
or the unknown in me?

Landmarks

Lord
we praise you
for the nature landmarks of our lives
   mist-laden hills from which your help comes
   shadowed valleys where we may walk without fear
   sun-blessed plains that stretch far
      with your magnanimity

Lord
we praise you
for the people landmarks of our lives
   opponents who force us to
      toughen our truth
      and
      acknowledge theirs
   friends who know us through and through
      and love us still and all
loved ones who are there
   wherever there is
   always there

Lord
we praise you
for the spirit landmarks of our lives
   laughs that trigger laughs
   tears that just keep coming
   longing that will not be stilled

I Will No Longer Ask Permission

I don't want to live
the next period of my life
to meet the expectations of
everybody else
but
to meet my own deepest needs

I will no longer ask permission
to disengage from duty
to others
long enough
to honor duty
to myself

Lord help me sift
selfishness
from self-love
help me honor
needs
over expectations
confirm me
or disconfirm me

I'm not sure what you want of me
and for me
but
I believe you are calling to me

in my wants
as in my oughts
in my needs
as in my obligations

help me connect what I want
with what you want

I'm Sorry

I'm sorry
  for offending people
  and then being hurt
  that they're offended
  and not caring
  or hoping
  quite enough
  to go and say
    I'm sorry

I'm sorry
  for forgetting the kind things
  and remembering the cruel things
I'm sorry
  for being angry
  at the wrong time
  and not
  at the right time
I'm sorry
  for holding grudges
  and hugging bitterness

I'm sorry
  for neglecting my friend
  who needs affection
I'm sorry
  for not consulting my colleague
  who needs respect

I'm sorry
   for being sarcastic to my wife
   who needs understanding
I'm sorry
   for being critical of my daughter
   who needs appreciation
I'm sorry
   for being sorry for myself
   who needs love.

O Lord, Enable Me

   it is taking more time
         energy
         heart
   than I thought would be necessary to
   heal

   others are nourshing me
   reaching out to me
   I need them
   maybe it's okay for awhile
   to be on the receiving end of
   encouragement

      O Lord, enable me
         to accept their kindness
         without apology
         or embarrassment

        enable me
        to accept your mercy
        without presuming
        or defending

   enable me
   to accept myself
   without put-down
   or put-on

        enable me
        to accept any I have hurt
        damaged in ways
        I cannot repair

        enable me
        to accept any who have hurt me
        or misunderstood me
        or judged me
        and keep a bitter spirit from me

O Lord, let me not wallow in self-pity
        nor simmer with resentment
        but pick up whatever is my burden
        and carry it

Make Me Ever Green

O Lord
Your kindness is new
every morning

I delight in the land
blooming ever green
the warm sun on my forehead
the yellow beauty
after a season of rain

Wipe away my tears

Renew the land of my life
Make me ever green

Warm my spirit

Heal the ache of yesterday
Bear me on wings of promise

Lord, Let Me

Where there is loss
        there is gain.
Where there is sorrow
        there is wisdom.

There is freedom
        only where there are limits.
There is forgiveness
        only where there are
betrayals.

Lord
let
me

Grieve my losses
Ponder my sorrows
Engage my limits
Acknowledge my betrayals

that
I
may

celebrate my gains
weather into wisdom
value my freedom
receive forgiveness

. . . *And Where We Cannot*

grant us grace
     to forgive
         and where we cannot forgive
     to forbear
         and where we cannot forbear
     to understand
         and where we cannot understand
     to accept

Falling Stars and Leaves

last night was cold, clear
stars immediate, diamond-sharp
in the bowl of a sky
   and then
      through the Milky Way
       a falling star

falling stars and leaves

this morning between the boughs
I saw the distant hills along the river
fog hanging low in the valley
a burst of blackbirds just after sunrise
the sun warming my face

where have all the leaves gone?

the time of falling leaves
when the mature colors
present themselves
mauve, russet, amber, plum

their leaves
fading
falling
uncovering boughs bare and real

the shape of the hills abides
the substance that is left
that endures
that holds out for what life means

life defines in the autumn
the gathering spirit ripens
in the seasoned flesh of the years
the bones appear
the face weathers
the fruit is borne

there comes a comfortable chill
to the night air
and harvest
draws
near